Hey You!

We need to talk!

LIZY CELESTINE

INDIA • SINGAPORE • MALAYSIA

ISBN 979-8-88935-894-7

Dedication

To my dear mother, who has always been my number one fan and supporter, even when my writing was nothing more than chicken scratch on a piece of paper (although it still is but just on a quality paper of Notion Press).

To my brother, who may have pretended to roll his eyes at my book talk, but secretly read every word I wrote. To my father, who may have pretended not to be interested in my writing, but was secretly marketing my book in his circle of friends.

To my future husband, who is still stuck on a tree or something, and to my future extended family, just so that you don't feel neglected.

To all my friends, family, and loved ones, who have been my beta readers, my critics, and my source of inspiration.

And to the aliens out there, if you're reading this, please don't abduct me. I've got more books to write and though I want to dedicate this to you guys, my mother says she won't sponsor this one if I don't dedicate it to her. But somehow, this book is dedicated to all of you, for without your support and encouragement, it would have never seen the light of day. Thank you for being the wind beneath my wings, and the stars in my universe.

Just kidding, this book is dedicated to my dogs, Cleo, Coco, and Charlie, because let's be real, they are the only ones who truly understand me.

Contents

About the Author

Meet Lizy Celestine, the author of "Hey You!"- the book that will have you questioning everything you thought you knew about life, love and the universe. Lizy is an aerospace engineer with an MBA and a bunch of certifications in psychology and somehow a successful entrepreneur, who at the young age of 29, got bored of the corporate world and decided to partially retire early to pursue her true passion - writing and being a smartass.

With her unique perspective as an innovator, educator, and successful entrepreneur, Lizy has seen the best and worst of the corporate world and has come out on the other side with a wealth of knowledge to share. As the founder of organizations imparting aviation education to prestigious universities, she has a unique understanding of what it takes to succeed in the fast-paced world of business. But she got bored with it all and decided to adopt a couple of pets and live a boring life and now she's trying to show others how to have fun.

Lizy likes to live in the clouds, just like Alexa, but

unfortunately, she's currently residing in Bangalore with her pets Charlie and Cleo, who helped glue this book together with their drool. Lizy speaks fluent sarcasm and sometimes uses English, Telugu, and Malayalam to make it sound better. She is the youngest oldie you could ever meet and if you plan on meeting her, please don't search for her office, because that's one place she never goes. Because, you know, the office is so last century.

As an education enthusiast, Lizy realized that she didn't study enough when she went to college, so she is now doing her M.Sc. in psychology after realizing that psychology is her passion now. She believes that understanding the human mind and behaviour is the key to understanding oneself and others. And it's not like she had anything better to do.

But don't let her credentials fool you, Lizy isn't your typical self-help author. She doesn't sugarcoat the truth or offer empty promises, instead, she offers a refreshing and unique take on self-help, with a heavy dose of sarcasm and humour. So, if you're looking for a self-help book that will make you laugh, think, and question everything you thought you knew, written by a person who knows how to be bored and wants to show you how to have fun with a little help from her pets, then go on. Read at your own risk.

Acknowledgements

Firstly, I would like to thank all the aliens for helping me with wonderful ideas whenever needed.

Thank you, Cookie, for reminding me every day about completing this book. Thank you, Choco Chip, for staying married to cookie even after a month and nagging him to do his job of reminding me about this book.

Thank you, Cat for listening to my crazy book ideas even at midnight, and for all those gossip and brutal truths that became a part of this book. Thank you, Jaadoo, for showing me that there is still magic in life. And thank you Wonder Woman, for all those wonders you created with your unicorn pen.

Thank you, Thalaiva, for taking care of my pets while I write this and for occasionally feeding them.

Most importantly, thank you Dr. Joy for all the therapies and pills that helped all these humans and aliens to remain calm while I finish this book.

And lastly, Thank you, Whiskey for reminding me that I'm still the boss and I can fire people. Most importantly, thank you, Mr. Bean and Mrs. Whiskers for teaching me how mean this world can be and you have no idea how grateful I am to have come across such life gurus like you all.

Yours truly,

Vampire

P.S: All the characters mentioned above are purely fictional, and any resemblance to anyone living, dead, or waiting to die is only incidental. The insults and sarcastic comments are purely intentional, though.

Preface

Welcome to "Hey You!" - the book that will have you questioning everything you thought you knew about life and the human experience in the most sarcastic way possible. It's like that book that tells you how to ask your insecurities and fears to go to hell in such a way that they look forward to the trip! You'd feel that everything you've known so far about life is just crap. It's like a wake-up call from the universe, telling you to stop settling for mediocrity and start living your best life.

You'll dive into the deep end of life's mysteries, such as "What's beyond life?" "Who am I?" and "What is the meaning of love?" (Hint: look at yourself in the mirror once before reading these.) You'll learn about the desirable desires that you never knew you had, but don't worry, I won't tell you how to achieve them.

You'll navigate the treacherous waters of the judgemental world and learn how to deal with insecurities, not by building confidence but by asking them to take a one-way trip to hell. You'll discover the truth about trust, that it's not trustworthy, and that's okay. You'll explore the reasons behind divorce, and learn that it's not just about incompatibility, but about realizing that marriage is the main reason for divorce.

You'll also dive into the harsh realities of life, such as betrayal and abandonment, and learn how to let go, not by finding balance but by just not giving a damn. You'll also learn about the differences between men and women, and you'll discover the ethics of modern society, which, let's be real, don't matter that much. And finally, you'll learn how to find satisfaction in life, or accept that you'll never find it and just settle for a life of mediocrity.

So, Hey You! if you're ready to have some fun, question everything, and discover the truth about life, this book is for you. It's not your typical self-help book, it's a sarcastic and humorous take on the human experience. So buckle up, and let's begin this journey of self-discovery and sending insecurities and fears to where they belong, together.

Foreword

As a practising psychiatrist, I've seen it all. The tears, the tantrums, the therapy pets. But let's be real, sometimes the best medicine is a good laugh. And that's exactly why I'm thrilled to introduce "Hey You!", a self-help book that will have you questioning everything you thought you knew about life, love, and the universe.

Written by Lizy Celestine, an aerospace engineer with an MBA and a successful entrepreneur, this book delves into all the important topics in life such as desirable desires, trust, the judgemental world, insecurities, happiness, trauma, grief, satisfaction, and true love, amongst others. But unlike other self-help books, this one is written in a sarcastic tone, because let's face it, life can be pretty ridiculous, and sometimes the only way to deal with it is by laughing at it.

Lizy doesn't sugarcoat the truth or offer empty promises, instead, she offers a refreshing and unique take on self-help, with a heavy dose of sarcasm and humour. It's the perfect blend of entertainment and education. And trust us, understanding others is overrated, you're better off just laughing at them.

"Hey You!" will help you navigate the complexities of life and relationships and find fulfilment and happiness. With Lizy's unique perspective and skills, she'll guide you on a journey of self-discovery, helping you to understand yourself and others better. It's like therapy, but cheaper and more entertaining.

And don't worry, if you're not a fan of self-help books, this one won't make you want to gouge your eyes out. In fact, it's so good, you might actually enjoy reading it. Who would have thought?

So, if you're tired of the same old "positive thinking" and "how to succeed" advice and you're ready for something different, "Hey You!" is the book for you. It's not your typical self-help book, but it's not like you're a typical person either, right?

And remember, if you don't like the book, you can always use it as a doorstop or a frisbee. It's multi-purpose. So, grab a copy, sit back, relax, and let Lizy Celestine guide you on a journey of self-discovery and laughter. And who knows, you might even learn something new.

Dr.Sampath Venkataswamy
MBBS, MD-Physiology
DNB -Psychiatry
Certified Positive Psychologist (University of Penn)
Professor at Windsor University

01

How Are You?

Hey there! How are you today? Wait, let me guess: you're probably thinking, "Oh great, another person asking me the age-old question 'how are you?' And as per usual, I'm supposed to say, 'I'm fine,' even if I'm feeling like a hot mess and my day has been a complete disaster."

Am I right? I know, it's such a mundane and cliché question, but it's one that we're all guilty of asking and answering daily.

"How was your day?"

"It was fine (except for the fact that I spilt coffee all over my new shirt, got stuck in traffic for an hour, and found out my dog ate my lunch. But other than that, everything was great)."

"How are you feeling?"

"I'm fine (just ignoring the throbbing headache and the fact that I'm overwhelmed and stressed out)."

"How's work?"

"It's fine (if you don't count the fact that my boss is a jerk and my co-workers are driving me crazy)."

Fine, fine, fine. We're all just a bunch of "fine" robots, going through the motions of daily life without really stopping to think about how we're actually feeling.

But let's be real, life isn't always "fine." Sometimes it's amazing, sometimes it's terrible, and most of the time it's somewhere in between. So why do we insist on pretending that everything is okay when it's not? Maybe it's because we don't want to burden others with our problems, or maybe it's because we're afraid to admit that we're struggling. Or maybe it's just because it's easier to say "I'm fine" than to go into a long-winded explanation of all the things that are going on in our lives.

Whatever the reason, it's time to break the cycle of "I'm fine" monotony. Next time someone asks you how are you? Don't be afraid, be honest. If you're feeling great, say so! If you're having a tough day, it's okay to admit it. And if you're somewhere in between, that's normal too. Let's stop pretending that everything is always "fine" and start being real with each other.

So, how are you today? Be honest. No more "I'm fine"

bull shit. Let's get real and start being authentic with each other. It may seem scary at first, but trust me, it's a lot more fulfilling than pretending to be "fine" all the time. Plus, it's kind of refreshing to hear someone admit that they're not okay once in a while. We're all humans, and it's okay to have bad days. So let's embrace our imperfections and be real with each other. It'll probably make us all a little happier in the long run.

02

Desirable Desires

Desirable desires deserve to be desired!

We all desire, and we keep on desiring one thing after another. As one desire fulfils, another pops up, and this goes on and on until the end of our lives.

Desire drives the world, and without hesitation, it's the only reason for our existence. Our desires make us who we are, our identity, our pride, and our ego. What we possess is what we have desired, and our life is a reflection of our desires.

But not all desires get fulfilled all the time, right? We tend to brood over those unfulfilled desires and we look for ways to fulfil them. That is the mere process where we lose our peace. Desires not only make our life but can break too.

Our happiness and sorrow solely depend on desires. Am I right? If our desire gets fulfilled, we feel happy, if not we are unhappy.

But we all want happier lives, don't we?

On one end of the spectrum, we have successful people who say "work hard to fulfil your desires, realize your dreams and be happy and successful." There are wide arrays of books that teach you how to work hard or smart and be successful.

On the other end of the spectrum, we have saints who say, "curb your desires, reduce your desires, give up everything, leave the worldly pleasures, and in that way you achieve happiness and peace."

But we don't belong to either! We are simply human beings living a mediocre life, chasing our dreams, and feeling contempt for the fulfilment of every tiny desire.

How do we achieve peace and happiness then? If peace attained only by those who fulfil all their desires, by those who curb their desire, what happens to us who are driven by tiny desires every day? Can't we be happy?

Yes, we can be! Happier than either of them to be precise!

It's just that we should desire desirable desires. How do we do that?

So far, all lives on this planet are controlled by desires

in one way or the other. We follow and pursue what we desire. But have you noticed something? Where do desires come from?

From the mind or the heart? From outside or from within?

Desires come from our hearts. So we call them our hearts' desires. Have you ever heard of my mind's desires? No, right? It's our heart that desires.

Where does this heart get its motivation for desiring though? From outside or from within our body?

Since the heart lies within the body, you might say desires come from within. But no.

It's from outside! Sounds strange, isn't it? We cannot desire what we have not known or seen or felt. Have you observed that? If our neighbour wears a good dress, immediately our heart desires something similar or even better. If our colleague gets a promotion, we desire a promotion or even a pay raise. If our friend buys a new car, we desire a better car, probably even a better model than our friend!

See, how our desires are stimulated by external forces. It's not entirely the external stimulus to be blamed.

Your desire is the result of your reaction to the external stimulus. If you would have seen that dress or car or promotion and just remembered that you don't need those at the moment, your heart wouldn't have locked in those emotional reactions and created desires.

It's because of your reaction, your desire popped up! You don't have to react to everything you see or be envious of every beautiful thing your friends or neighbours own!

All you have to do is work together with your heart's desires, rather than letting desires take control of your life or taking control of your own life by suppressing those desires.

Let's say, your heart says you should get a better car than your neighbour, but your mind immediately steps in and does some math and says NO! You cannot afford that! Then again, the heart says, let's try taking a loan, you can repay in no time. Mind says it's difficult to manage your savings with huge loans. And then heart steps in with some other excuse.

In this never-ending battle, sometimes the mind wins and you may never thank it, but sometimes the heart wins and you will blame your mind for not giving you a caution before investing all your life's savings in a car!

It's always mind vs. heart! But no one is the boss here! Kindly understand that. Your heart, your mind, and your body must be in sync with each other.

They must be working together with you, and for you, rather than working against each other. Your heart's desires should be taken into consideration after consulting with your mind once! Your mind and heart should both be involved in your decision-making process.

That way, you analyze your present socio-economic conditions and then take a step forward towards fulfilling the desire. Rather than desiring and running behind fulfilling those desires all your life.

You know what, there will be a moment both your mind and heart give a heads up when you desire something, that's what I call desirable desire.

And desirable desires are bliss to be fulfilled. Take one step at a time, you will never regret it! And mindful decisions help to create organized goals, and reaching each goal and stepping up one step higher every time boosts your self-confidence to such an extent, that you no longer feel like a slave, but the master of your life!

When you only desire desirable desires that can be fulfilled, where is the room for sorrow or disappointment? It's pure happiness!

Desire desirably and you will realize peace lies within you. Living happily or peacefully should not be the ultimate goal of our life, it should just be a process of life.

03

Feelings We Call Love

We all know the word "love" and use this word deliberately to express our feelings or emotions of fondness, like, and affection. Love is a universal language. It might mean different to each one of us, and we might perceive it in different forms. We have never come across the actual definition of love, although it's debatable, let's have a look at what I found.

"Love is a complex mix of feelings, actions, and beliefs associated with strong feelings of affection, protection, warmth, and respect for others. Love can be seen as the bond between two people or as the feeling one person has for another, but it can also be viewed as a virtue that expresses human kindness, compassion, and affection—a selfless, loyal, and benevolent concern for the well-being of others."

Now let's assume this definition applies to most of us. In this case, love, as defined above, is an action expressed through feelings of affection, protection, and warmth.

But over time, why does affection turn into a weakness, protection into possessiveness, and warmth into a mere gesture? Why does caring for and supporting each other become an inevitable and burdening responsibility, while respecting the significant other's opinion is mistaken for dependence?

However, not all relationships express the same form of love or have the same feelings associated with them. There are distinct types of love, and they are associated with different feelings and emotions. Let's look at the basic forms of love, such as romantic love, familial love, platonic love, and self-love. Each type of love has its own characteristics and can be expressed in different ways.

Romantic love is a strong affection that exists between two people who are romantically attracted to each other. This type of love is often characterized by passion, desire, and deep connection.

Yet, ironically, romance has become a culture and is the most desirable trait we look for in a partner. If romantic love is the ultimate expression of our love for one another, why do we tend to seek romance as a compatibility measure even before falling in love with that person?

Romantic love is an intense and powerful emotion that

promotes healthy relationships. But these days, it can evoke fears of vulnerability and rejection. In all modern relationships, one of the partners has to be romantic enough to keep the other in the relationship if not, there is a fair chance that the relationship is likely to end. Isn't fear of rejection, fear of losing a partner, and fear of being abandoned that keeps relationships going these days, rather than love, trust, and support?

Family love refers to the love between family members, such as parents and children, brothers and sisters, and extended families. This type of love is often characterized by strong feelings of protection, loyalty, and responsibility.

Do our families these days still have the same bonding and love? Do our children know their roots? Do they spend enough time with grandparents and other extended family members and relatives? Forget about what we teach our children, what were we taught as a child? Instead of strong feelings of protection, loyalty, and responsibility for one another, we were taught how to compete with other siblings and to always be one step ahead of others. It's often a tradition in Indian families to compare one with another. For most of us, our worst enemy was the sibling who scored more marks or the one who won more medals. Most of our childhood was spent trying to score better and be the best at everything.

We were constantly compared with other siblings, and our success purely depended on scoring better or doing better than our siblings or cousins. Instead of loyalty, we often find our family members worrying about relatives' success and celebrating their failure. It doesn't matter whether we do well or not, it's sufficient if our relatives don't do better than us.

Divorces have become the new culture and child abandonment is the new trend. Families are split and children grow up to be lonely, self-centred, and success driven. When we teach our children the importance of being successful in life or a career, we often forget to teach them how important failures are and how to learn from our failures and mistakes. We were taught a lot about individuality, leadership qualities, and independence that we lost touch with how to be a supportive team player, or how to ask for help when needed without feeling ashamed. Most of us these days talk to therapists more than we talk to our family members. Ironically, we feel that an unknown therapist can understand us better than known family members; such is the bond between us and our family members.

Platonic love is the type of love that exists between friends. This type of love is characterized by strong feelings of affection and support, but it is not necessarily romantic or sexual.

But how hard do we find it to accept the fact that there can be a healthy relationship between two genders without romance or sexual inclinations? How many of us can accept our spouse or partner having a good relationship with a friend of a different gender without feeling threatened? It has become such a taboo and a way beyond our sane minds to accept a healthy relationship, that we convince ourselves and call it a "crush."

Self-love is the love that we have for ourselves. It is important to have a healthy sense of self-love and self-worth, as it allows us to value and respect ourselves and our own needs and desires.

With a healthy sense of self-love and self-worth, our generation took a step ahead and we do anything and everything to make ourselves happy and satisfied, whether or not it affects our relationships, family, friends, society, environment, or nation. We tend to be selfish, greedy, and self-centred and we call it self-respect. We act compulsively and do anything that comes up in our mind, be it good or bad, and we safeguard ourselves by saying "I accept myself for the way I am" or we call it "respecting one's own needs and desires." Should self-love outgrow our sense of morals and ethics?

As for whether love decreases over time, it is important to note that all relationships and emotions change and evolve. It is normal for the intensity of romantic love to change and evolve as a relationship progresses. However, this does not necessarily mean that love decreases or fades away completely.

In fact, many people believe that love can grow and deepen over time, as long as it is nurtured and cultivated. However, we are used to throwing away broken things rather than fixing them. The same goes for our relationships as well. We tend to lose interest and break off ties with our loved ones over silly matters that, we ignore the very idea of working together towards making things better again.

We live in a world where happiness depends on the number of likes on social media and success is measured by the amount of money, cars, flats, or shares we hold. The only way we communicate with others is through social media, and we express our feelings through DPs or status updates. Similarly, we call it a relationship or we say we are being loved only when we get whatever we desire from the other person, be it attention, gifts, money, or even time. The day either one of us loses interest is the day we call it quit and end that so-called happily ever after...

Yes, we all know this, and we all agree with whatever that's said above. Where is the problem then? We call a pencil a pencil only until it fulfils the required conditions of being a pencil, like a wooden case with graphite, so on and so forth. What happens when the case is of some other material and there is an ink refill instead of graphite? Do we still call that a pencil? No. We call it a pen.

Similarly, if love is all about being generous, compassionate, kind, loyal, affectionate, and all that's said in the definitions above, isn't it time to introspect about the emotions and feelings that we have for others that we call love? Either the definition of love should be changed according to what is practised as love these days, or we should change ourselves and understand the true meaning of love. Which of these do you think needs to be implemented? Change the actual definition of love or change our self-made definition of what we call love. If we are to follow what the definition says, then how many of you are in love? How many of you can say, you have been loved?

04

Can Trust Be Trustworthy?

It's often said that loyalty is hard to find, but trust is easy to lose. If someone is loyal to you, does that mean that person is trustworthy too?

Maybe, right? Because loyalty and trustworthiness are often closely linked, as loyalty is often based on trust. But can a loyal person be trusted? And can a trusted person be loyal? I know it's a bit confusing and for some of us, it might even question everything that we have believed in so far. Loyalty and trustworthiness are two different traits. But strongly dependable and closely knit.

Loyalty refers to a strong feeling of support or allegiance to a person, group, or cause. It involves being faithful, reliable and committed to something or someone, and it is often seen as a positive quality in personal and professional relationships. Trustworthiness is also seen as a positive quality and refers to the belief in the reliability, truth, ability, or strength of someone or something. When someone is loyal and trustworthy, they are generally seen as dependable, which can strengthen relationships and build trust over time.

It is important to remember that loyalty and trustworthiness are not the same things, and it is possible for someone to be loyal without necessarily being trustworthy. It is also possible for someone to be trustworthy without necessarily being loyal, as trustworthiness is about being reliable, truthful, and dependable, regardless of the level of loyalty one has for a particular person, group, or cause.

It's better understood with a few examples of how one might be loyal without necessarily being trustworthy:

A loyal spouse may be committed to their relationship, but they may not always be reliable or truthful in their communication with their partner. It's undeniable that in a relationship, we are loyal to each other, but do we trust our partner with our phones unlocked even for a minute?

Our pets are loyal to us, and we are loyal to our pets too. Do we trust our pets with babies when alone? Can our pets trust us after we lure them and swap their favourite treat for medicine or pills?

We all have friends, and we are loyal to each other and our friendship. Can we trust a friend when he says he will be back with the bike in ten minutes? Can we trust our most loyal girlfriends with a secret?

These examples might seem funny, silly, and I'm sure, sarcastic and humorous. But when we closely observe, it's more alarming than funny. We are living in a world where trust exists only in mistrust.

Our phones need passwords, our purchases need receipts, employers need contracts, families need joint accounts, marriages need certificates, and our homes need security cameras!

We cannot walk our pets without a leash, and our children cannot play outside without supervision. A child is never yours until you have a birth certificate, and your home is never yours until you have property documents. We aren't graduates until our degree certificate says so, and we haven't died until a death certificate says so.

A girl child cannot be left alone with a male family member/relative, and our maids or nannies cannot be trusted with our homes. Water is drinkable only if the packaging says so, and we are our countrymen only if our passports say so.

Mistrust has become the new normal now. Is it because of the way the world is now or is it because of how we perceive the world? Let us be honest, don't we all feel it's safer not to trust anyone with anything? Is it because the other person cannot be trusted, or is it that we don’t trust our own judgement about the other person’s trustworthiness?

Can we at least trust ourselves? Can we trust ourselves with our feelings, cravings, mood swings, thoughts, and impulsiveness?

Can the word “trust” be trusted? Is trust trustworthy?

05

The Judgemental World

Am I tweeting too much these days? I must be jobless and free all day.

Am I not tweeting much? I must be depressed. Did I respond to your text within a minute? I must have been waiting for your text eagerly.

Did I not respond to your text for a while? I am rude and maybe, I'm ignoring you.

Did I dress well for your party? I'm stealing your thunder.

Did I dress casually for your party? I'm a disgrace and party inappropriate.

Indeed, people often make judgements about others based on several factors, such as their appearance, behaviour, actions, and words. These judgements can be based on personal biases and preconceptions, as well as societal norms and expectations.

If someone has tattoos or piercings, they may be judged or labelled as being rebellious or unconventional.

If someone is overweight, they may be judged or labelled as being unhealthy or lazy.

If someone is very thin, they may be judged or labelled as being anorexic or bulimic.

I have never met a single person on earth who successfully went through their day without being judged. The irony is that we don't even leave our gods without passing judgement. If we recall, Lord Rama had to send Maa Sita back to the woods just because some random person passed judgement on Sita Devi's character after being under Ravana's clutches.

Similarly, in the Mahabharata, Duryodhana makes judgemental comments about the Pandavas, saying that they are not worthy of ruling because they are not of royal birth. This led to a war between the Pandavas and the Kauravas.

We are judged based on our appearance, such as our clothing, hairstyle, or other physical characteristics.

"You're always wearing bright colours; you must be really happy."

"You're always wearing all black; you must be depressed."

"You're always wearing high heels; you must be trying to impress someone."

"You're always wearing flip-flops; you must not care about your appearance."

"You're always wearing your hair in a ponytail; you must be too lazy to style it."

"You're always wearing make-up; you must be insecure."

"You're always wearing sweats and a t-shirt; you must not care about your appearance."

"You're always wearing expensive clothes; you must be trying to show off."

We are judged based on our actions, such as choices, decisions, or behaviours.

"You're always smiling; you must be fake."

"You're always serious; you do not have a sense of humour."

"You're always agreeing with others; you must be a

pushover."

"You're always disagreeing with others; you must be difficult to work with."

"You're always speaking up; you must be trying to show off."

"You're always quiet; you do not have anything important to say."

"You're always helping others; you must be a people pleaser."

"You're always focusing on your own needs; you must be selfish."

We are judged no matter what. Whether we do something or not. There is no possible way to avoid judgements. Let me share more examples of how we are judged.

Did you go shopping or on a trip with your friends? You must have heard these:

"You're always spending money on luxury items; you must be selfish."

"You're always saving money; you must be a miser."

"You're always taking out loans; you must not be good at managing your finances."

"You're always giving money to charity; you must be trying to show off."

"You're always investing in stocks; you must be greedy."

"You're always buying second-hand items; you are not able to afford new things."

"You're always paying for everything in cash; you must not have a credit card."

"You're always using your credit card; you must be earning too much."

Do you have friends who are well off? You are sure to hear one of these:

"You're always hanging out with popular people; you are trying to be like them."

"You're always hanging out with unpopular people; you do not have any other friends."

"You're always hanging out with people who are different from you; you are not able to fit within your own group."

"You're always hanging out with people who are the same as you; you must be trying to fit in."

Did you just go on a date? You better know who you are:

"You're always dating successful people; you must be a gold digger."

"You're always dating less successful people; you do not value success."

"You're always dating older people; you must be trying to find a sugar daddy."

"You're always dating younger people; you must be trying to find a trophy partner."

Do you give importance to relationships and spend time talking to people?

"You're always talking to your partner; you must be clingy."

"You're always talking to your friends; you must not have any other interests."

"You're always talking to your family; you must be a mamma's boy/girl."

"You're always talking to your boss; you must be sucking up."

"You're always talking to your co-workers; you must not have any other friends."

Or do you just stick to your phone?

"You're always texting; you must not have any real-life social skills."

"You're always on social media; you must be addicted."

"You're always on the phone; you must be rude and disrespectful."

We live by judgement. We always judge and are judged. If you felt bad hearing any of these comments at any point in time, and if you have felt insecure in life, and wished for a world where you feel accepted, then maybe you should start becoming the change you wish to see in the world.

Forget about what others say. Just remember what you say to yourself standing in front of the mirror every day, trying those outfits, striving for a perfect winged liner, or trying to fold your t-shirt sleeves to pop your biceps. You spend countless hours questioning yourself if you are looking good, if your body is in shape, if your make-up is perfect, or if your outfit is good enough for the occasion.

Haven't you asked yourselves these questions at any point in your life? If you feel you are up to your social standards, well and good, your mirror is a friend. What if you had to encounter failure or what if you feel you are not up to social standards? This is what you say to yourself:

"I'm not smart enough to understand this concept."

"I'm too overweight to try skin-fit clothes."

"I'm not good enough to be a part of this group."

"I'm not talented enough to succeed in this field."

"I'm too old/young to be able to do that."

"I'm not attractive enough to be with someone like him/her."

"I'm not well-dressed enough to fit in here."

"I'm not qualified enough to hold this position."

We judge ourselves even before someone else judges us. We become such critics that we no longer accept ourselves. Every time we encounter a judgement, instead of being disheartened and losing confidence, if we could accept ourselves, and move on, I believe, we would be living life on our terms rather than based on others' opinions.

If we could accept ourselves, criticize less, and understand more, we would not only be at peace with ourselves but also with everyone around us. We aren't computers to be with same specifications and standards. We are humans. We are born different; our lives are different and I'm sure our destinies are different too. Then, why try to fit in when you are born to stand out?

06

Is dealing with insecurities a way to build confidence?

Alright, let's talk about insecurities. Because let's be real, they're the worst. They're like that annoying little voice in the back of your head that just won't shut up, telling you that you're not good enough, that you don't belong here, that you're not pretty/smart/talented/fill-in-the-blank enough. Ugh, it's the worst. And unfortunately, it seems like everywhere we look, businesses are trying to exploit our insecurities for profit. They want us to believe that we need their product or service to fix whatever it is we're insecure about. They tell us that with their miracle cream, we'll finally have perfect skin. With their latest workout programme, we'll finally have the perfect body. With their newest gadget, we'll finally be cool and popular. It's like they're saying, "hey, don't worry about all that stuff you're insecure about, just buy our stuff and everything will be peachy." But here's the thing: our insecurities are not something that can be fixed with a magic potion or a quick fix. They're an ongoing battle that we have to face every day.

But here's the good news, we don't have to let our insecurities win. We don't have to let them hold us back or define us. We can choose to be confident and self-assured, even if it's not the easiest thing to do. And yes, it might take some work and some time, but it's totally worth it. Because when we're able to overcome our insecurities, we open up a whole world of possibilities. We can pursue our dreams and goals without fear holding us back. We can be ourselves and not worry about what other people think. We can be happy and fulfilled, even if we're not "perfect."

So how do we do it? How do we kick our insecurities to the curb and start living our best lives? Well, it's not going to be easy, but here are a few tips:

Identify your insecurities: The first step is to figure out what's causing you to feel insecure. Is it your appearance? Your intelligence? Your relationships? Your career? Once you know what's at the root cause of your insecurities, you can start to work on addressing them. And no, buying that "miracle" cream or "revolutionary" workout programme probably won't fix the problem. Sorry to disappoint.

Reframe your thinking: Our insecurities often stem from negative thought patterns or beliefs that we have about ourselves. By reframing these thoughts and replacing them with more positive ones, we can start to see ourselves in a more positive light. For example, instead of thinking "I'm not good enough," try thinking "I'm doing the best I can and that's all that matters." Or instead of thinking "I'm not pretty enough," try thinking "I am beautiful in my own unique way." See, that wasn't too hard, was it?

Practice self-compassion: It's easy to be hard on ourselves when we feel insecure, but this only serves to make us feel worse. Instead, try to be kind to yourself and remind yourself that everyone has insecurities. It's okay to not be perfect – in fact, it's completely normal! And besides, who wants to be perfect anyway? That sounds like a lot of pressure.

Focus on what you can control: It's easy to get caught up in things that we can't control, like other people's opinions or the way we look. But by focusing on the things that we can control, like our actions and our attitudes, we can start feeling more in control of our lives and be confident about ourselves. Instead of worrying about things like our appearance or what other people think of us, we can focus on being the best version of ourselves. We can work on being kind, compassionate, and helpful to others. We can focus on learning new things and developing new skills. By doing these things, we can start feeling more confident and secure about ourselves, regardless of what anyone else thinks.

Seek support: It can be helpful to talk to someone about your insecurities, whether it's a friend, family member, or professional. Just having someone to listen to and offer a different perspective can be really helpful. It can also be helpful to surround yourself with supportive, positive people who lift you and encourage you to be your best self. These people can be a great source of strength and inspiration when you're feeling insecure.

So there you have it, a few tips for dealing with insecurities. I know it's not easy, but I promise it's worth it. By working on your mindset and practising self-compassion, you can start feeling more confident and self-assured. And while businesses will always try to tap into our insecurities as a market, it's up to us to decide whether or not we want to buy into their promises. We have the power to choose how we feel about ourselves, and that's a pretty amazing thing. So don't let your insecurities hold you back any longer. You are worthy, you are capable, and you are enough. Now go out there and kick some butt!

07

What's the reason for divorce? Marriage!

Well, well, well. It seems like marriage is becoming more and more of a joke these days. It's like, as soon as things get tough, it's easier to just throw in the towel and file for divorce. No more sticking it out and working through problems, as our ancestors did. No, no, no. We're too much modern and enlightened for that.

But let's take a step back and examine some of the ridiculous reasons people are getting divorced these days. I mean, seriously, some of these things are just ridiculous. For example, I've heard of people getting divorced because they didn't like their spouse's cooking. I mean, come on, people. Is that really a valid reason to end a marriage? How about the couple who divorced because one of them snored too loudly? Or the couple who divorced because they couldn't agree on what colour to paint the living room? The list goes on and on.

Now, let's compare this to marriages in the olden days. Back then, people really knew how to stick it out and make their marriages work. They didn't have the option of just walking away at the first sign of trouble. No, they had to work through their problems and find a way to make it work. And you know what? A lot of them did. They ended up having long, happy marriages that lasted a lifetime.

So what happened? Why are marriages falling apart left and right these days? Well, I think it's because we've lost sight of what's really important in a relationship. We've become too focused on superficial things, like material possessions and social status. We're not willing to put in the work and effort it takes to make a marriage work. We're too quick to throw in the towel and move on to the next thing.

But it doesn't have to be this way. We can turn things around and start building strong, healthy marriages again. It just takes a little bit of effort and a whole lot of commitment. Here are some tips for making your marriage work:

Communicate openly and honestly: This is probably the most important thing you can do TO strengthen your marriage. Make sure you and your spouse are on the same page and can talk about your feelings and concerns without fear of judgement or criticism.

Make time for each other: With busy schedules and demanding careers, it can be easy to put your marriage on the back burner. But it's important to make time for each other and prioritize your relationship. Make date nights a regular part of your routine and find ways to connect and bond with your spouse.

Be willing to compromise: No relationship is perfect, and there will always be times when you and your spouse don't see eye to eye. It's important to be willing to compromise and find common ground to move forward.

Seek help when you need it: If you're having problems in your marriage, don't be afraid to seek help. Whether it's counselling or just talking to a trusted friend or family member, getting an outside perspective can be incredibly helpful in working through issues and finding solutions.

And let's not forget about the societal pressure to get married as we get older. It's like society has this unspoken rule that you need to be married by a certain age or you're somehow incomplete. And don't even get me started on the pressure from our parents. They seem to think that getting married will magically fix all of our problems and turn us into upstanding citizens. "Oh, he's just a troubled boy, he'll straighten out once he gets married." Yeah, because marriage is the answer to all of life's problems, right?

But seriously, folks. It's time to stop letting society dictate our lives and start making decisions that are best for us. Just because we're getting older doesn't mean we have to get married. And just because someone is having a little bit of trouble doesn't mean that marriage is the answer. It's important to think about what we really want and what will truly make us happy, rather than just following the crowd or trying to please others.

So let's make a pact, shall we? Let's stop letting society dictate our lives and start making our own choices. Let's not be afraid to buck the trend and do what's best for us. And let's stop believing that marriage is the answer to all of life's problems. It takes more than a piece of paper and a fancy wedding to make a happy, healthy relationship. It takes hard work, dedication, and a whole lot of love.

So, should you get married? That's a tough question and one that only you can answer. Marriage is a big commitment, and it's not for everyone. But if you do decide to tie the knot, make sure you're doing it for the right reasons and that you're committed to putting in the work to make your marriage thrive. Don't just jump into it because it's the "thing to do" or because you feel like you should. Take the time to really think about it and make sure it's the right decision for you.

08

Happiness

Happy Birthday!! Happy Sunday!! Happy Holidays!! Happy Anniversary!! Happy, Happy, Happy! Why do we all look for happiness in everything? Why do we always wish for happiness?

Because clearly, we have nothing better to do than sit around and contemplate our navels all day. I mean, who has time for all that happiness jazz when we have emails to answer, meetings to attend, and errands to run?

But seriously, happiness is a feeling that we all strive for, even if it does feel elusive and out of reach at times. And while it's easy to get caught up in the hustle and bustle of modern life, it's important to remember that happiness is not just an emotion or feeling. It's a state of mind or a way of being that is characterized by a sense of well-being and fulfilment.

So, now that I've given you the rundown on happiness, I have a few personal questions for you. When was the last time you did something just for the fun of it, without worrying about the result or what others might think? When was the last time you caught up with a friend or loved one and really focused on the present moment, rather than checking your phone or thinking about your to-do list? When was the last time you took some time for yourself and did something that brings you joy and relaxation, like reading a book or going for a walk?

These may seem like small, insignificant actions, but they can have a big impact on our overall happiness and well-being. So, don't be afraid to make time for these things in your busy life. They may not pay the bills or get you that promotion, but they will bring you a sense of joy and fulfilment that is worth more than any material gain.

So, how can we go about cultivating happiness in our super busy lives? Here are a few tips:

Find activities that bring you joy and fulfilment: This could be anything from hobbies and creative pursuits to volunteering and helping others. Just try to squeeze them in between your back-to-back meetings and laundry sessions. For example, if you love cooking, try setting aside some time on the weekends to whip up a tasty meal. Or, if you're a nature lover, make an effort to go for a hike or spend some time in the garden.

Cultivate positive relationships: Research has consistently shown that people who have strong social connections are generally happier and healthier than those who are more isolated. So, make an effort to spend time with loved ones, cultivate new friendships, and reach out to others when you need support. Just be sure to schedule all that socializing between your early-morning gym sessions and late-night work sessions. For example, try setting aside some time each week to catch up with a friend over coffee or make an effort to attend social events and meet new people.

Practice self-care: It's important to take time for ourselves and prioritize our own well-being. This can be as simple as taking a few minutes to meditate or go for a walk or making time for activities that bring us joy and relaxation. Just try to fit it in between your packed schedule of grocery shopping, carpooling, and dog walking. For example, try setting aside some time each day to do a quick meditation or yoga practice, or make a conscious effort to unplug from technology and relax.

Find a sense of purpose and meaning: When we have a clear sense of what we want to achieve and why it matters, we are more likely to feel fulfilled and happy. This can be achieved through setting goals and working towards them, as well as finding ways to give back and make a positive impact on the world. Just try not to let all those pesky work deadlines and family obligations get in the way. For example, try setting some long-term goals for yourself and breaking them down into smaller, more achievable steps. Or, consider volunteering your time or resources to a cause that you care about.

By finding activities that bring us joy, cultivating positive relationships, and finding a sense of purpose and meaning in our lives, we can cultivate a sense of lasting happiness that can help us to thrive and flourish. So go out there and chase your happiness, my friends! Don't let the demands of modern life get in the way of finding a sense of purpose and meaning. Choose to be happy, and don't let anyone or anything stand in your way.

Or, you know, just keep on hustling, and maybe, happiness will come to you eventually. Just don't forget to pause and smell the roses (or the coffee, depending on your preference) along the way. Happy chasing!

09

Finding True Love

"There is more hunger for love and appreciation in this world than for bread." – Mother Teresa

We all have felt that hunger for true love at least once in our lifetime.

We all have longed for "the one" who could fill the emptiness in our hearts and make us whole and complete.

We all have searched for that "destined one" who is out there somewhere waiting to meet us. Who would just come along and fit in as a missing piece of our life's puzzle?

No one is an exception. For years we have been searching for that deep, soul-stirring, life-changing, heart-throbbing, magical, always and forever, happily ever after kind of love.

I haven't found one, though! Have you?

After years of study on relationships and a lot of brainstorming sessions within myself, a few questions remain unanswered.

What is true love? Can we ever find it? When every single soul in this world is longing for it, why hasn't anyone found it? Is true love a myth?

My heart still says no! It's not a myth.

But in reality, we all might have felt that "the person who was my Mr. /Ms. Right is not anymore now. The same person who gave so much love, affection, and care is now giving so much hurt and pain."

This isn't something unexpected. Every single day in our relationship we all have lived with the fear that one day we might be cheated on, lied to, taken for granted, disappointed, or hurt. But still, we all try to work on our problems and live with the hope for a better and love-filled tomorrow.

One fine day I happened to realize the reason for our problem, i.e., lack of true love.

The reason we all fail in finding true love is not that we chose the wrong "Mr /Ms. Right". It is because we understood the love of our "Mr. / Ms. Right" in the wrong way!

Over the years, we all have modernized the word "love" so much that we have lost its true meaning. Love as we see in modern days is shielded by possessiveness, ego, mistrust, anger, jealousy etc.

As long as we support our feelings towards our partner with these aliments like possessiveness, ego etc. It's not just one person, every person whom we choose will seem like the wrong one.

The secret of true love:

The secret to finding "the one" lies in understanding the real meaning of true love.

True love is boundless and universal!

True love is not about finding the right human being. It is a state of being!

True love only comes with a deep sense of understanding. To experience true love in your life, you should first start understanding. Understanding yourself first and then understanding your partner.

Once you start trying to understand yourself, you understand what you like. What makes you feel insecure in your relationship? How much do you trust your partner? When was the first time you lied to your partner and what made you do so? Which aspect of you makes him/her angry? Why does your partner complain about this behaviour in you? What do you lack in your relationship now? What is making you unhappy?

So, once you understand who you are, you realize that you are not the person you thought you were. Your inner self is different from what you show the outer world. Once you reach this point, it shouldn't be difficult for you to understand that all human beings on earth are different from each other. God has not made any photocopies. Only originals, distinctly different from each other.

Now, do you realize that you and your partner are also two different souls trying to be one?

Once you have understood yourself, try to understand your partner.

What does your partner like? Where is he /she happiest? What excites your partner? Which food does your partner love? What does your partner like doing in his/ her free time? What was one aspect of his /her life your partner always wanted you to understand? Where in life does your partner need you not to judge but instead just forgive or accept? When was the first time your partner did something that upset you and what was your partner's explanation for it? Was your partner understood and forgiven, or do you still feel you don't understand him/her well?

The fact is that you two are entirely different souls trying to be together. It's natural that your behaviour, food taste, choice of friends, dressing sense, and the way you look at things, entirely differs from your partner. But this lack of a simple understanding that you are different from each other is the only and main source of your problem.

Your partner is entirely different from you. Accept your partner the way he/she is. Appreciate your partner's uniqueness. Understand his/her passions. Love your partner just the way she/he is.

There is only a thin line between love and possessiveness.

True love doesn't demand change in the other person.

True love requires you to accept the other person not for what you want him/her to be but for what he/she is.

Your husband likes spending time with his friends. Will you welcome him home happily once he comes back from watching a late-night movie with his friends? No, you say, it hurts, he doesn't love me enough, he is not paying attention to me, he is taking me for granted. That's where your doubt started and trust is falling apart. The next time he is late, you flood him with phone calls, and messages, and try to grab his attention just to make sure he only thinks of you even when he is with friends. This is possessiveness. Every strong relationship needs possessiveness but more than a certain limit will cause imbalance. If it exceeds the limit, you become tough with him. You think he only belongs to you and has to be with you. If that doesn't happen, you become arrogant and threaten him saying that "If you don't stop talking to your friends, I will leave you. Choose either me or your friends." This is an obsession; it is like poison to any healthy relationship.

Understanding is the key.

Instead, understand that he feels happy watching a movie once in a while with his friends. Appreciate it and feel happy because you know your loved one is happy there. Don't you feel happy seeing your one-year-old kid playing with all his friends? Do you tell your kid that he has to be only with you all the time? No, because you understand that your kid needs some playtime with friends. Similarly, when you start understanding your husband you will feel happy that he is happy there doing something he likes. Shopping might make you happy, but your husband might find it boring. So when you go out shopping with your girlfriends, you don't expect your husband to object to it and act against your wish. Right? The things that make him happy may not make you happy. Because you two are different and unique in your own way. Accept it and love it. So that your partner will also learn to understand you and accept you the way you are. Once your partner understands that you are trying to be understanding and accepting, he/she would also try to understand your desires and appreciate your opinions and respect your decisions.

Imagine what a miracle could happen in your relationship if you and your partner start understanding each other, respecting each other's needs, and decisions, and being happy with each other despite your different tastes and opinions.

The taste of perfection.

A perfect relationship isn't when the husband comes home early every day from work, buys you flowers, or takes you out on a date. It is a perfect relationship when you understand your husband is having a good time with friends and you let him enjoy himself while you watch your favourite series with your girlfriends happily, which otherwise you wouldn't be able to enjoy as it's going to be a sports channel on TV after he arrives!

A perfect romantic date with your husband doesn't always have to be with two straws in one coke while sharing the same pizza. It can also be when you sip your favourite coffee engulfed with its aroma while you let your husband frizz up a little with his favourite "drink" and you two engage in a heartfelt conversation. A lot can happen over a drink too.

The perfect couple is not the one who always stays together wherever they are. The perfect couple is the one who stays together despite where they are.

That is the essence of true love. To find your true love, don't search for "the one," just search within yourself and understand the one you already have. Once you understand, you will realize that the one you already have, is actually "the one".

Start Understanding! Start loving truly! Your Mr./Ms. Perfect is just next to you.

Once you re-discover your true love, don't forget to write to me about your experiences.

10

Am I Worth It?

Hey there, your fabulous human being!

Do you ever catch yourself thinking?

“Am I worth it?”

“Why am I not good enough?”

“What is wrong with me?”

“Why can’t I do things right?”

“What is the point of trying, I’m going to fail anyways.”

“Why do I even bother?”

I know, I can see that quirky smile. Like hell yeah! You must have thought this many times in your life, or maybe you encounter these feelings daily. Be it work or in personal or social life.

How many times have you thought of wearing that peppy dress to a party, but you never wore because you feel you don't look good in it, or you can't pull it off well like the other model-looking friends or colleagues?

How many times have you thought of going on to that stage and giving your opinion, but never went because you felt your opinion doesn't matter? Or someone would make fun of you?

Have you ever stopped yourself from attending appraisal meet or corporate parties just because you feel you aren't welcome there and you are not good enough like your other colleagues?

How many times have you written a message and deleted it after sending it? How many unsent emails about your new project or idea are lying in your drafts, that you haven't gathered the courage to send it yet?

How long have you been holding on to that love letter you wrote but couldn't give because you felt you aren't good enough for him/her? Or you felt you don't have to give because you will be rejected anyways?

Has the fear of failure stopped you from trying or doing things you always wanted to do? Have you ever felt that you are worthless, rejected and not appreciated or loved?

Did you ever ask yourself "Am I really worth anything?" If yes, then well, let me tell you – the answer is a big, fat YES. You are worth it. You were, and you are.

Let me tell you one thing straight – you are a unique and valuable individual, simply by virtue of being alive. You deserve love, respect, and the opportunity to pursue your dreams and goals.

Remember, you are strong, capable, and worthy. Believe in yourself and your abilities, and you can accomplish anything you set your mind to. And if all else fails, just remember – you are a warrior. You are living this hell of a life and are still doing well.

It's completely normal to have moments of self-doubt and to question your worth, but I want you to know that you are worthy and valuable, just as you are.

I know it can be tough to believe in yourself when you're going through a tough time, but I want to encourage you to take a moment to reflect on your strengths and accomplishments.

Remember that day when mommy kissed you and said she was proud of you? Remember that day when you got your first bike and took your proud dad on a ride? Remember those days when your friends came asking for advice? Those days when the whole class clapped for you when you performed. Or when your dad smiled at you for doing something well? These are things that make you unique and special, and they are worth celebrating.

We all are unique in our own way. It's just that as we grow older, we forget our uniqueness and try to join the crowd. And it's quite common to feel lost. I know it's easy to get caught up in comparing ourselves to others and feeling like we aren't good enough. But let me tell you, everyone has their own insecurities and struggles. So don't try to be someone you are not – just be the best version of yourself. And don't give up, even if you feel like you are facing a never-ending series of challenges (like those impossible levels in that one video game you can't beat).

It's time to ditch self-doubt and remember all the amazing qualities that make you who you are. You have your strengths, skills, and talents, and these are what make you special and worthy. Don't let anyone else tell you otherwise – even if they are better than you at something (I'm looking at you bullies, watch out) at the end of the day, no one can be better at living your life than you.

It's also important to take care of yourself, both physically and mentally. This includes getting enough sleep, eating a healthy diet, and exercising regularly. If you're struggling with depression, anxiety, or thoughts of suicide, please don't hesitate to reach out for help. It's okay to not feel okay all the time, and it's important to seek support when you need it. You don't have to go through this alone.

So keep pushing forward and remember that you are worth it. You have the potential to do remarkable things and make a difference in the world. And hey, if anyone tries to tell you otherwise, just remind them that you are a unique and fabulous human being – and that's worth a million bucks. You are amazing, and you have so much to offer the world.

And stop deleting messages after sending them. And send those unsent emails to your boss or colleague about your new ideas. You are worth listening to. So don't hold yourself back and type and send that message!

11

Grief

We all have lost something that we have deeply cared for, right? For some, it is a loved one or a family member or for others, it could be a pet. Even the loss of a job, loss in business, failure, or even the end of a relationship can cause grief.

Grief can be a real bummer, can't it? It's one of those emotions that just sucks the joy right out of life. And if you're anything like me, you're probably thinking, "Great, just what I needed. Another unpleasant emotion to deal with."

It's like the ultimate buzzkill, isn't it? Just when you think you've got everything under control, bam! Grief comes along and messes everything up. It's like that annoying relative who always shows up uninvited and overstays their welcome.

But here's the thing: grief is a completely normal and natural response to loss. It's a sign that we cared deeply about the person or thing that we've lost, and that we're experiencing a deep sense of emotional pain. And even though it may feel impossible, it is possible to overcome grief.

If there is anything I would suggest to you, that would be to appreciate grief with all the best memories of what it has left you with. Ever wondered, why we enjoy music when we are happy and tend to understand the lyrics when we are sad? Grief does the same thing. It's up to you whether you want to process your grief by enjoying the best memories or making more painful memories that would surpass the best memories you have with your lost one.

In the meantime, here are a few things that might help:

Talk to someone: Whether it's a friend, a family member, or a therapist, talking about your feelings can be really helpful. It can be cathartic to just get everything off your chest, and having someone there to listen can be comforting. Just make sure you choose someone who won't judge you or try to fix your feelings. We all need a good venting session now and then. You can even talk to your teddy bear. I tried it, and it works! Teddy Bears are so much better than people anyways, right? But just make sure you close your doors while talking to your teddy. You don't want to end up at a therapist after choosing teddy over a therapist to talk to in the first place.

Take care of yourself: Grief can take a physical and emotional toll on your body, so it's important to take care of yourself. Make sure you're eating well, getting enough sleep, and taking breaks when you need them. And don't be afraid to treat yourself every once in a while. A little bit of ice cream or a bubble bath can do wonders for the soul. I'd even recommend shopping or a spa visit.

Find ways to honour the person or thing you've lost: Whether it's writing a letter, creating a memorial, or doing something special in their honour, finding ways to remember and honour the person or thing you've lost can be therapeutic. And if you're feeling really brave, you can even do something silly or fun in their memory. Sometimes laughter is the best medicine. If you're dealing with the loss of a job, you can even try writing a hate letter to the boss who fired you but just don't send it. Just burn it. I meant the letter, not your boss!

Find ways to move forward: This might mean finding new hobbies or activities to do or finding ways to get back to your normal routine. It's important to find ways to move forward and not get stuck in grief. And hey, if all else fails, you can always turn to the trusty old "fake it till you make it" strategy. It might not be the most authentic way of dealing with grief, but it can be effective in the short term.

So there you have it. Grief may be tough, but it's something that we all have to deal with at some point in our lives. Just remember to be kind to yourself, take it one day at a time, and remind yourself that this too shall pass. It might pass like a kidney stone, but it will pass.

12

Betrayal

Wow, betrayal! How fun! Nothing like having the rug yanked out from under you by someone you trusted and cared about. I mean, seriously, who doesn't love feeling hurt and confused? It's like a party in your brain!

But hey, at least it's not coming from an enemy, right? That would just be too easy. No, it's always the people we love and trust who manage to stick the knife in the deepest. How thoughtful of them!

But seriously, despite how much it sucks, betrayal can actually be a pretty valuable experience. I mean, sure, it sucks at the moment. You're allowed to feel angry, hurt, and bitter. Go ahead and wallow for a bit. But eventually, you're going to have to pick yourself up and move on. And when you do, you might be surprised at how much stronger and more resilient you are because of it.

Betrayal can be one of the most difficult and painful experiences we face in life. It can shake our trust in others, make us question our judgement, and leave us feeling hurt, confused, and alone. But it's important to remember that betrayal is a normal part of life, and it's something that we all experience at one time or another.

It's natural to feel angry, hurt, and bitter when we are betrayed. We may feel like we've been wronged and that the person who betrayed us should be held accountable. But it's important to try to move beyond these emotions and find a way to heal and move forward. Betrayal can be difficult, but ultimately a growth-promoting, experience. It can force us to confront difficult emotions, challenge our assumptions about the world, and ultimately make us stronger and more resilient.

One way to begin the healing process after a betrayal is to try to understand why it happened. It's important to remember that people who betray us are not necessarily bad. They may have made a mistake, acted out of fear, or been driven by their own insecurities or pain. By trying to understand the motivations behind the betrayal, we can begin to let go of our anger and resentment and find a way to forgive.

Forgiveness is not about excusing or condoning the betrayal. It's about letting go of our anger and resentment and finding a way to move forward. Forgiveness can be difficult, especially when the betrayal was particularly hurtful or damaging. But it's important to remember that forgiveness is not about the person who betrayed us; it's about ourselves. By forgiving, we can let go of the negative emotions that are holding us back and find a way to heal and move on. What I mean to say is, forgive! Not because they deserve forgiveness, but because you deserve peace.

First things first, it's important to take some time to wallow. Go ahead and treat yourself to a pint of ice cream (or three), watch some tearjerker movies, and listen to sad love songs on repeat. Especially if it's about your ex or that colleague or friend you trusted, it's okay to feel angry, hurt, and bitter – your ex /colleague totally deserves it.

But eventually, you're going to have to pick yourself up and move on. And when you do, there are plenty of funny (and cathartic) ways to get back at them for their betrayal.

For example, you could:

Create a playlist of upbeat, empowering songs to help you move on (bonus points if they're songs that your ex/ colleague hates).

Share memes and GIFs about betrayal and heartbreak with your friends to make them laugh (and to make you feel less alone).

Practice your best "gloat face" in the mirror, because when you finally run into your ex /that colleague and they see how amazing you're doing without them, you're going to want to look good.

It's also important to remember that betrayal is a normal part of life. No one is perfect, and we all make mistakes. The key is to learn from those mistakes and use them as an opportunity to grow. By doing so, we can build stronger, healthier, and more meaningful relationships with others.

I know that betrayal can feel overwhelming and impossible to overcome, but I promise you that you are stronger and more resilient than you realize. You have the power to heal and move forward from this experience. It won't be easy, but it will be worth it. Believe in yourself and in your ability to overcome this challenge. You've got this. And remember, I said forgive! Not forget! I meant not to forget the lesson learnt.

13

Success and Failures

Hey there, feeling down because you've experienced a few failures in life? Oh no, how terrible! I mean, it's not like everyone experiences failure at some point or anything. It's not like the most successful people in the world have failed countless times before achieving their goals. No, no, that couldn't be it.

I mean, seriously though, failure is a completely abnormal thing that only happens to you, right? You're the only one who has ever lost a job or performed poorly on an exam. You're the only one who has ever felt like you're not reaching your full potential or not sure what your capabilities are. Nope, no one else has ever felt that way.

Well, since you're the only one who has ever experienced failure, I guess it's time to just give up and crawl into a hole, right? Oh wait, that's not helpful at all. Let's try this instead: Accept that failure is a normal part of life. Everyone fails at some point. It's important to accept that failure is a natural part of the journey towards success. Just look at all the successful people who have failed before achieving their goals:

J.K. Rowling: Before becoming a household name in the Harry Potter series, J.K. Rowling was a struggling single mother living on welfare. She was rejected by multiple publishers before finally finding success with the Harry Potter books.

Steve Jobs: Steve Jobs was fired from Apple, the company he co-founded, in 1985. He went on to start several other successful companies, including Pixar Animation Studios

Walt Disney: Walt Disney was fired from a newspaper job because he "lacked imagination." He went on to create one of the most successful entertainment companies in the world.

Albert Einstein: Einstein's theory of relativity was rejected by multiple scientific journals before it was finally published. He went on to become one of the most famous and influential scientists in history.

So why don't we take a look at better ways to deal with failures? Here is some piece of advice that might work.

Learn from your failures: Take some time to reflect on what went wrong and what you can learn from the experience. This will help you avoid making the same mistakes in the future. And hey, at least you'll have a good story to tell at parties. "Remember that time I bombed that job interview/exam/presentation? Good times."

Don't beat yourself up: It's easy to get caught up in negative self-talk after a failure, but this will only hold you back. Try to be kind to yourself and remember that everyone makes mistakes. You're only human, after all. Stay positive: It can be tough but try to stay positive and keep a growth mindset. This will help you stay motivated and focused on your goals. Plus, it's way more fun than being a grump all the time.

Keep trying: Don't give up! Remember that success often requires persistence and perseverance. And if all else fails, you can always try that whole crawling into a hole thing. Just kidding, don't do that.

Now, who doesn't want success right? After all, self-help books are for that unending lessons on how to succeed, isn't it? So let's talk about success. Success might mean different things to different people, but there are a few common themes that tend to emerge. Success often involves setting and achieving goals, finding fulfilment and happiness in your work, and making a positive impact on the world. So, how do you achieve success? Here are a few tips:

Set clear goals: It's important to have a clear idea of what you want to achieve. This will help you stay focused and motivated. Just don't set your goals too high or you might end up in a failure spiral.

Work hard: Success often requires a lot of hard work and dedication. Don't be afraid to put in the effort. But also remember to take breaks and have some fun along the way. Success isn't all work and no play, after all.

Seek feedback and learn from others: Surround yourself with people who will support and challenge you. Seek feedback from others and be open to learning new things. Just don't take criticism too personally. It's all part of the process.

Stay positive and keep a growth mindset: A positive attitude and a willingness to learn and grow can go a long way in helping you achieve your goals. And hey, it's a lot more fun than being a grump all the time.

Be resilient: Things won't always go according to plan. It's important to be resilient and adapt to change.

So there you have it, some tips for dealing with failure and achieving success. Remember, failure is a normal part of the journey towards success, and that's how we learn and grow. And if all else fails, just remember that you can always crawl into a hole and hide. Just kidding, don't do that. Keep going and never give up!

14

Trauma

It still haunts you, isn't it? You want to forget it but you can't. Sleepless nights and nightmares that wake you up, a pounding heart, and a restless body. Emotionally drained and feelings of hopelessness, right?

Well, that's what trauma can do to us.

I know that the mere thought of it brings up a plethora of emotions that are hard to navigate, but I want you to know that you are not alone in this. Whether it's physical, emotional or psychological trauma, it can leave us feeling lost, confused, and unable to cope. It's like a dark cloud that seems to follow us everywhere we go, and it can feel impossible to escape.

Trauma is a difficult and painful experience that can have a lasting impact on a person's emotional and mental well-being. Have you ever experienced something so distressing or shocking that it has left you feeling unable to cope or move on? If so, you are not alone, as trauma affects many people.

There are many different types of traumas, including physical trauma, emotional trauma, and psychological trauma.

Physical trauma can occur as a result of an accident, injury, or violent attack. This type of trauma can result in physical injuries and can also lead to emotional and psychological trauma.

Emotional trauma is caused by a deeply distressing or disturbing event, such as the loss of a loved one, a divorce, or a major life change. This type of trauma can result in feelings of sadness, grief, and despair, and can also lead to emotional and psychological difficulties such as depression and anxiety.

Psychological trauma is caused by an event or series of events that are deeply distressing or disturbing, such as sexual or physical abuse, or experiencing a natural disaster. This type of trauma can result in a wide range of psychological symptoms, including anxiety, depression, and PTSD (Post-traumatic stress disorder).

But I know that it's not just about the kind of trauma, it's personal, it's the traumatic event that haunts you. Have you ever lost someone you loved? Have you ever been a victim of violence? Have you ever experienced something so terrible that it feels like it's taken a part of you? I know it's not easy, but I want you to know that you are not alone in this. And the pain, the hurt, the trauma you are feeling, it's understandable and valid.

Trauma can have a wide range of after-effects, including physical symptoms such as headaches and chronic pain, as well as emotional and psychological symptoms such as anxiety, depression, and PTSD. Trauma can also lead to difficulty with trust, feelings of worthlessness and shame, difficulty in relationships, and difficulties with memory and concentration.

But here's the thing, healing is possible. And I know it may not feel like it right now, but you have the strength and resilience to overcome this. There are many different ways to deal with and overcome trauma, including therapy, counselling, and support groups.

And I know it's not easy, but just in case you need it, here are some tips that may help you on your journey to overcome trauma:

Seek professional help: It is important to talk to a therapist or counsellor who is trained to help individuals deal with trauma. They can provide you with a safe space to process your feelings, help you identify and challenge any negative thoughts and behaviours that may be holding you back from healing, and provide you with tools to manage the symptoms of trauma.

Practice self-care: Taking care of yourself is crucial during the healing process. Make time for self-care activities that you enjoy, such as exercise, meditation, or spending time in nature. It's also important to get enough sleep, eat a healthy diet, and avoid drugs and alcohol.

Take control of your thoughts: Trauma can affect how you think about yourself and the world around you. Try to focus on the present moment and practice mindfulness techniques such as meditation or deep breathing. It can help you let go of the past and have a more positive outlook on life.

Allow yourself to feel the emotions: Trauma often causes intense emotions. Trying to suppress or ignore these emotions can prolong the healing process. Instead, allow yourself to feel the emotions, but remember to practice self-care, try to understand the emotions and process them.

Be kind to yourself: Permit yourself to take the time you need to heal. Be patient with yourself and don't compare your journey to others. Healing takes time and it's a different process for everyone.

Keep in mind that healing is not linear: It's important to remember that healing is a journey, and it's not always a straight path. It may take time and there will be setbacks, but with self-compassion, patience, and the support of others, you can get through this.

I want you to know that you are not alone, and you are strong. You are capable of healing and moving forward, even in the face of unimaginable trauma. Just keep fighting and know that a brighter future is ahead. And remember, it's okay to not be okay. You deserve to heal, and you deserve a chance to lead a happy and fulfilling life.

15

Understanding is the Key

Do you ever wonder why your spouse leaves the toilet seat up?

Do your parents drive you up the wall with their nagging?

Do you sometimes look in the mirror and think, "Who the heck am I, and why am I here?"

If you answered yes to any of these questions, then congratulations, my friend! You're in the right place.

First of all, let's talk about understanding ourselves. This can be a tricky business, especially when you consider all the voices in your head are constantly vying for attention. You've got the voice of reason trying to make logical decisions, the inner child throwing tantrums, and that one voice in the back of your head whispering, "you know you want that second helping of ice cream." But when you start to understand your own thoughts and emotions, you can start to make sense of the chaos and make better choices. And isn't that what life is all about? Making better choices so you can eat more ice cream?

When it comes to understanding others, it's important to remember that no two people are exactly alike. And that's a good thing! Can you imagine a world where everyone was exactly the same? BORING! But it can be tough to understand why someone else sees things so differently than you do. Like, for example, why your spouse thinks it's perfectly acceptable to leave their dirty socks on the coffee table, but you find it revolting. But when you take the time to understand where they're coming from, you may find that it's not about the socks at all, but about entirely something else. And suddenly, the socks don't seem so bad.

Of course, understanding others is not always easy, and sometimes it can feel like banging your head against a brick wall. But remember, it's all worth it in the end. When you understand someone else, you're able to communicate more effectively and build stronger, more meaningful relationships. And isn't that what life is all about? Strong relationships and meaningful communication or is it just about the ice cream?

Let's address the elephant in the room - understanding ourselves and others can be a real pain in the butt. I mean, do you ever wonder why your spouse leaves the toilet seat up? Or why do your parents drive you up the wall with their nagging? It's enough to make you want to pull your hair out. But, as science tells us, understanding oneself and others is essential for building healthy relationships, both personally and professionally.

When you understand yourself, you're able to set boundaries, communicate effectively, and make better decisions. And when you understand others, you're able to empathize, compromise, and build deeper connections. Studies have shown that more self-aware people tend to be more resilient and better able to cope with stress. Additionally, research has found that more empathetic people tend to have better relationships, both personally and professionally.

But let's be real, understanding others can be a real pain in the butt. Take parents, for example. They're always telling you what to do, how to do it, and when to do it. But as you grow older, you start to realize that they're just trying to protect you and give you the tools to navigate this crazy world. And maybe, just maybe, they're not always wrong.

And what about our spouses? Ah, the joys of marriage. The late-night fights over whose turn it is to do the dishes, the constant bickering about the thermostat setting, the endless debate over which TV show to watch. But as you grow older, you start to realize that these arguments are just a small part of the big picture. And that, in the grand scheme of things, you'd rather spend your life arguing with the person you love than with someone you don't.

So, what's the point of all this? The point is that understanding oneself and others take time, patience, and a whole lot of sarcasm. But if you're willing to put in the work, you'll be rewarded with stronger relationships and a better understanding of the world around you.

In all seriousness, understanding oneself and others is an ongoing process, and it can be difficult, but it's also fun and rewarding. It's like a puzzle, you keep trying to fit pieces together, but at the end of the day, you know it's all worth the effort. With patience, a bit of sarcasm, and a dash of humour, you'll be well on your way to creating deeper connections and a better understanding of the world around you.

That's why I want to offer you some practical tips for understanding oneself and others:

Practice active listening: When you're in a conversation with someone, focus on what they're saying and try to understand their perspective, instead of just thinking about what you're going to say next.

Be open-minded: Try to be open to new perspectives and experiences, it will help you understand and accept others more.

Be patient: Understanding oneself and others takes time and patience. Don't get discouraged if you don't get it right the first time.

Take a break: Sometimes, it's necessary to step back and take a break when you're feeling overwhelmed by your emotions or by trying to understand others.

You might not know the answers to everything, but taking the time to understand yourself and others is key to making the most of your time on this earth. By making the effort to understand yourself and others, you'll be setting yourself up for a happier, healthier, and more fulfilling life. And who wouldn't want that? So go out there, be curious, be kind, be patient, and most importantly, have fun with it! Understanding oneself and others is an ongoing journey, and you never know what you might discover about yourself and the world around you. And always remember, sarcasm is the highest form of intelligence.

So, take a deep breath, put on your sarcasm goggles, and get ready to embark on the wild and wacky adventure of self-discovery and understanding of others. Because in the end, isn't it all worth it?

16

Men Are from Mars and Women Are from Venus

Why do women always want to talk about their feelings?

What do men think about when women are shopping?

Why do men always need to watch sports?

What do men think when a woman is asking for directions?

Why do men always have to fix things?

What do women think when a man is crying?

Why do women always have to be on time?

I'm about to blow your mind with some earth-shattering truths about the differences between men and women.

"Why are men from Mars and women from Venus?"

Well, it's quite simple really. Men are from Mars because they're always trying to avoid conflict and responsibility, just like how Mars is the planet that's furthest from Earth. And women, well, they're from Venus because they're the complete opposite, always trying to create drama and chaos, just like the intense heat and volcanic activity on Venus.

But seriously folks, the truth is that men and women are different, and that's a good thing! Can you imagine a world where everyone was the same? It would be so boring. We need men to be men and women to be women to make the world a more interesting place.

Now let's talk about the real elephant in the room: the difficulties of understanding the opposite gender. Why is it so hard? Well, let's take the example of Indian culture. For example, in India, men are supposed to be strong and emotionless, while women are supposed to be weak and submissive. When a man shows vulnerability or cries in public, he is considered weak and not masculine, or a woman is considered not fit for a leadership position if she displays her emotions at work. These stereotypes limit the expression of emotions and behaviour of individuals, which is not fair and healthy for any society. But, who really made these rules?

It's commonly assumed that men are interested in things like cars, sports, and technology, while women are more interested in fashion, beauty, and home decor. This stereotype is often perpetuated in media and advertising, leading many people to believe that these interests are exclusive to one gender or another. But in reality, many men love fashion, while many women love cars and technology.

We presume men are more direct and to the point, while women are more emotional and indirect. This stereotype can lead to misunderstandings and frustration, as men may feel like women are being unnecessarily vague and women may feel like men are being insensitive. But in reality, communication styles can vary greatly from person to person, regardless of gender.

It's important to remember that these stereotypes are just that: stereotypes. They are not based on facts, and they do not apply to every individual. By recognizing and challenging these stereotypes, we can begin to see people for who they really are, rather than who we think they should be based on their gender.

But let's not forget the importance of appreciating our differences and coexisting in the world. After all, without men, who would fix things around the house and ignore their partner's feelings? And without women, who would nag about everything and force their partners to watch sappy romantic comedies?

By understanding and appreciating the opposite gender, we can begin to break down the barriers that keep us from truly connecting with and understanding one another. We can start by challenging our own biases and stereotypes and be open-minded to new ways of thinking and different perspectives.

So, let's all raise a glass to the men and women of the world. May we continue to make life interesting, frustrating, and endlessly entertaining. And remember: men are from Mars, women are from Venus, but at the end of the day, we all live on the same planet, "Earth."

17

Ethics, Do they still matter?

Welcome to the ethical train wreck that is 21st-century society. I know, I know, it's a tough pill to swallow. But don't worry, we're all in this together. We've all lost our moral compass at some point or another. It's like we're all playing a game of ethical hot potato, passing off responsibility, and just trying to not get caught doing something wrong. But honestly, it's getting harder and harder to keep up with what's right and wrong these days. It's like the rules of the game keep changing and no one bothers to send out the updated rulebook. It's like we're all playing a game of ethical Jenga; one wrong move and everything comes crashing down.

Oh, and let's not forget about the little things, like when we're stuck in traffic and suddenly it's perfectly fine to drive on the shoulder to get ahead, or when we're running late and it's okay to push our way past others to get to where we need to be. Because who needs basic manners and common courtesy when we have places to be, right?

Or, how about when we're at the grocery store and we decide to sneak an extra item into the "10 items or less" line because, well, it's not like anyone's really counting, right?

And let's not forget the granddaddy of all ethical dilemmas: the age-old question of whether or not it's okay to sneak a peek at the answers during a test. Sure, it may give you an unfair advantage, but hey, everyone else is doing it, so it's not really cheating, right?

And let's not forget the times when we throw trash on the street or spit on the road because, well, someone else will clean it up, so it's not really our problem, right?

But the most hilarious and sarcastic of them all, would be when people are on social media and posting about their workout or about eating healthy, but meanwhile, they're secretly eating a whole pizza by themselves. Because, as we all know, abs are made in the kitchen, but pizza is made for the soul.

You might be wondering, "Why do we need to talk about this? I already know what's right and wrong." Well, my dear friends, you might be surprised at just how easy it is to stray from our moral compass in today's world.

Let's start with a little history lesson. Back in the good

old days (you know, when dinosaurs roamed the earth), people had a pretty clear understanding of what was right and wrong. Of course, there were always going to be some bad apples, but for the most part, society knew that things like stealing, cheating, and being cruel to others were wrong. Fast forward to today, and it seems like the lines between what is considered ethical and moral behaviour are blurrier than ever.

Take, for example, a social media influencer who promotes products they don't even use just because they get paid, or a celebrity who is caught in a scandal but still manages to keep their sponsors, or even worse, politicians who are caught in a corruption case but still get re-elected. It seems like these days, people are more concerned with getting ahead and making a quick buck, regardless of who they step on in the process.

But why is this a problem? Well, for starters, when we don't hold ourselves and others accountable to certain ethical standards, it leads to a slippery slope of moral decay. Before you know it, society becomes a free-for-all where everyone is out for themselves and no one cares about the well-being of others. This can manifest itself in many ways: increased crime, a lack of trust in institutions, and a general sense of cynicism and hopelessness.

And it's not just adults who are affected by the erosion of ethics and values. Children are watching and learning from us every day. If they see us cutting corners and taking shortcuts, they will likely do the same. But if we teach them the importance of honesty, kindness, and fairness, we can help create a future generation of responsible, compassionate, and ethical citizens.

So, what can we do to stem the tide of moral decay? The first step is to take a good, hard look at ourselves and our actions. Are there areas of our lives where we could be doing better? Are there habits or behaviour patterns that we need to change?

Next, we need to hold ourselves and others accountable. Speak up when you see someone acting in an unethical or immoral way. It might be uncomfortable, but it's important to call out bad behaviour when we see it.

We should also make an effort to understand and internalize the values that are important to us. It's one thing to know that honesty is a value that you should uphold, but it's completely another thing to actually live that value every day.

All of these examples might seem small and insignificant on their own, but when we add them up, they paint a pretty disturbing picture of where our society is headed.

It's time to take a step back and re-evaluate the choices we make daily. We owe it to ourselves, others, and future generations to strive for a more ethical and values-based society. So, let's all do our part, and remember, if all else fails, just pretend like your mother is watching and act accordingly.

18

Abandonment

Busy life, eh? Work from the office, work from home, and work on Sundays too. It's getting difficult to manage ourselves, right? And managing and caring for someone dependent on us is even more hectic. Getting a nurse or caretaker to care for our loved ones seems easier, isn't it?

We even feel proud these days that we have chosen the costliest old age home for our parents, and we did the best thing by putting our old pet to sleep. We just saved that pet from suffering! What a great deed!

Well, folks, it's time to face the harsh reality that we all must confront one day: old age. Whether it's our parents or our pets, they will all eventually grow old and need our care and attention. But the question is, will we rise to the challenge, or will we simply turn our backs on them and abandon them like yesterday's trash?

It's a sad fact that as our loved one's age, they are unable to take care of themselves, they are often abandoned by those who were once closest to them. Whether it's children neglecting their ageing parents, or pet owners abandoning their animals when they can no longer care for them, turning our backs on those who need us the most is a common occurrence.

The truth is, as our parents' age, they become more and more dependent on us. They may need help with basic tasks like bathing, dressing, and cooking. They may need assistance managing their medication or doctor's appointments. And as their minds and bodies deteriorate, they may become increasingly forgetful or confused. But instead of rising to the challenge and caring for them as they have cared for us, we often choose to ignore them, pushing them out of our lives and into nursing homes or other long-term care facilities.

The same is true for our pets. We bring them into our lives as adorable little balls of fluff, and we fall in love with them. They become members of our families, and we promise to take care of them for their entire lives. But when they grow old and sick and their once boundless energy is replaced by the need for constant care, we find ourselves unable to handle the responsibility. So we give them away or drop them off at a shelter, hoping someone else will take them in.

The feeling of being abandoned by loved ones is heart-wrenching. It's a feeling of betrayal, of being cast aside when we need them the most. For ageing parents and pets, it can be especially difficult, as they have a limited ability to understand why they have been abandoned and often feel confused and lonely.

The truth is, caring for ageing loved ones and pets is hard work. It requires patience, dedication, and a willingness to sacrifice our wants and needs for the sake of those we love. But the rewards of that care are immeasurable. The love and gratitude of an ageing parent who knows they are not alone, the loyalty and devotion of a pet who has been given a second chance at life, these are things that money can't buy.

It's easy to turn our backs on those who can no longer benefit us in the way they once did. But true love is about being there for someone, no matter what. And in the end, it's the love we give and receive in our lives that truly defines us as humans. And those who abandon their loved ones in their time of need are not only missing out on that love but also missing out on the opportunity to show what truly defines us as humans: to be empathetic, selfless, and loving.

It's a hard thing to take care of an ageing parent, but it's an even harder thing to watch them slowly die in a care home. It's a hard thing to take care of an ageing pet, but it's an even harder thing to watch them suffer and eventually die alone. But it's the hard things in life that make us who we are. And in the end, it's not an easy path that we'll be proud of.

It's important to remember that our loved ones, both human and animal, deserve our care and compassion, not just when they can benefit us, but always. And in the end, it's the love we give and receive in our lives that truly defines us as humans. It's the hard things in life that make us who we are, and caring for our ageing loved ones, whether they be parents or pets, is one of the hardest things we will ever do. But it's also one of the most rewarding. It teaches us empathy, selflessness, and the true meaning of love.

It's easy to take the easy way out, to neglect our ageing loved ones and push them out of our lives. But in doing so, we miss out on the opportunity to show them the love and care they deserve. We miss out on the chance to make a difference in their lives, brighten their days, and make them feel valued and loved. We miss out on the chance to make memories with them, memories that will last a lifetime and will be cherished long after they are gone.

It's never too late to make amends and show our loved ones the care and attention they deserve. Whether it's visiting an ageing parent in a nursing home or adopting an older pet, the little things we do can make a big difference in their lives. And in the end, it's the love we give that truly defines us as humans.

19

Harsh Realities of Life

Oh boy, where to begin? You're really selling the "harsh realities" of life, aren't you? Eating, drinking, working, and sleeping. How tedious, how absolutely dreary! I mean, who wouldn't want to spend their days toiling away in a meaningless job, coming home to stare blankly at the TV, and then just repeating it all over again the next day? Yawn. But hold on, before you give up on life altogether, let's think about this for a second. Are you really going to let the monotony of daily life dull your sense of wonder and possibility? Are you really going to waste this one shot at existence by just going through the motions?

Here's a thought: why not see things in a new light? Why not find a job that you're truly passionate about? One that aligns with your values and allows you to make a positive impact in the world? Suddenly, going to work every day becomes something to look forward to, rather than a chore to be endured. Or consider the time you spend with loved ones. We all have relationships that are important to us, whether it's with a partner, family members, or friends. But it's not enough to just be around these people; it's also important to make an effort to build deeper connections with them and appreciate the small moments that make those relationships special.

Another important aspect is finding balance in life. Taking time to engage in hobbies and activities that you truly enjoy, whether it's playing a musical instrument, reading, travelling or volunteering in your community. These things provide a sense of fulfilment and can give you a sense of perspective on life. And you know what, I think the real "harsh reality" here is the attitude you've got. Life is too short to waste it on negativity and cynicism. Why not try seeing things in a new light? Why not set some goals, chase your passions, and make the most out of every moment?

Embrace the journey, not just the destination. You only get one shot at this life, so make it count! Because if you don't, then what's the point? Of course, it's important to remember that we all have different perspectives on life, and what one person may see as a harsh reality, another person may find to be a source of joy and fulfilment.

Take the story of someone who has been working at a large corporation for years, but realizes that they're not truly fulfilled by their job and that their daily routine is not making them happy. They start to question themselves and rethink their priorities. Eventually, they decide to leave their job and start their own business, doing something they're truly passionate about. This person's experience illustrates how a shift in perspective can lead to a more fulfilling life.

Or, someone who has been working in a high-stress, high-pressure job for years. They have a lot of success and accomplishments in their career but realize that they're not happy and their mental health is suffering. They decide to take a sabbatical to travel around the world and volunteer in underprivileged communities. They find that the balance they found while travelling and giving back is what gave their life purpose and real meaning.

Another scenario could be of a person who has been working hard all their lives but finds that they've missed out on other important things in life like spending quality time with their family or friends. They realize that it's not just about achieving success professionally, but also about having a balanced life and having meaningful connections with others. They make a conscious effort to spend more time with their loved ones and make the most of the time they have with them.

Lastly, you could take the example of someone who's been living in a small town for most of their life and feels like they're stuck in a rut, but finds that by travelling, reading, and taking up a new hobby, they discover new perspectives and experiences that they never thought were possible. This brings them a new sense of purpose, fulfilment, and perspective on life.

As you can see from these examples, by questioning ourselves, re-evaluating our priorities, and being open to new experiences and perspectives, we can find greater fulfilment and purpose in our lives. Remember, life is not just about going through the motions; it's about making the most of every moment and every opportunity. Don't be afraid to question yourself; take control of your own happiness, and above all, have fun. It's about understanding what makes you happy and fulfilled, and making sure that you're living your life in a way that aligns with your values and passions.

And let's be real, life is not always going to be easy. There will be obstacles and difficulties that you'll have to overcome. But that's okay! These challenges are what make life interesting, and it's through overcoming them that we grow as individuals. And speaking of challenges, it's also important to remember that finding fulfilment in life is not always a linear journey. There will be ups and downs, and there may be times when you feel lost and uncertain. But that doesn't mean that you're on the wrong path. Sometimes, the most meaningful experiences come out of the most challenging moments.

So, don't let the "harsh realities" of life get you down. Remember that it's all about perspective, and try to see things in a new light. Find a job that you're passionate about, build deeper connections with loved ones, engage in hobbies and activities you truly enjoy and make sure that you're living your life in a way that aligns with your values and passions. Embrace the journey and the challenges, and most importantly, have fun! Because, let's be real if you're not having fun, what's the point?

20

Let Go!

Still, sending "thinking of you" texts to your ex at 3 a.m.?

Can't seem to throw away that old teddy bear from your ex?

Still holding on to that "I quit" letter for your old job?

Can't bring yourself to give away that dress you bought for the wedding that never happened?

Still, stalking your ex on social media?

Are you collecting dust in your closet, holding on to clothes that no longer fit you but "one day" you'll fit into again?

Still, have that picture frame of your ex on your nightstand?

Unable to part with the key to your old house, despite having moved on?

Still, talking to your ex-coworkers and updating them on your life despite quitting the job?

Still, holding on to that "I'll never forget you" note your ex gave you?

You know, it's funny, people always say they want to move on and be free but they're always holding on to something that's holding them back. Whether it's an old relationship that's long since ended, a job that they hate or a dream that they know will never come true, we all have something that we just can't seem to let go of.

I mean, are you one of those people? Holding on to something that's not working out for you? Or someone who's not good for you? Isn't it like holding on to a hot potato, the longer you keep it in your hands, the more it burns, but the moment you let go, the burning sensation goes away, and you're free to move on with your life? But I know it's hard to let go of something or someone that has been a part of your life for so long; it's like a part of you is missing, but trust me, it's better to let go of something that's holding you back than holding on to it and sacrificing your own happiness.

When we hold on to something that's no longer serving us, it can be a huge weight on our shoulders, affect our emotional and mental well-being, and prevent us from reaching our full potential. It can be difficult to see the bigger picture when we're stuck in our own thoughts, but imagine how much happier, and more fulfilled you would feel if you were able to let go of the things that are holding you back.

So, what are you holding on to? An old relationship that ended badly? A job that you can't stand? A dream that you know will never come true? Take a moment and think about why you're holding on– is it really worth it? Holding on to something that's causing you pain and heartache, sacrificing your own happiness and well-being for it?

It's important to understand that letting go doesn't mean that you're giving up; it's about moving on and making room for new things and new opportunities to come into your life. It's about choosing to let go of what no longer serves you to make space for something better.

So, how do you let go? Well, it's not easy, and it's different for everyone, but here are a few ideas that may help:

Write down what you're holding on to and why you're holding on, then read it and ask yourself, "is it worth it?"

Surround yourself with positive and supportive people who can help you let go and offer perspective.

Make a plan to move on and put it into action, it can be something small like unsubscribing from an ex's social media or something bigger like finding a new job.

Give yourself time, letting go takes time and patience, don't put pressure on yourself to let go overnight.

Remind yourself of all the things that letting go can bring you: freedom, happiness, and progress.

Practice self-care and engage in activities that make you feel good, like exercise, meditation or journaling; it helps to release the pent-up emotions and negative thoughts that may be holding you back.

You may find yourself struggling with a mix of emotions during this process, like sadness, anger, guilt, and even relief, that is normal and it's ok to grieve and feel these emotions. But also remember that it's not just about letting go of the thing or person, it's also about letting go of the expectations, the what-ifs, the plans, and the memories that come along with it. It's a process of self-growth, self-discovery, and healing, so take it one day at a time.

Why wait? Let go! Flush it like you know where it belongs, and move on!

21

The Quest for Satisfaction

Satisfaction, ah yes, that elusive feeling that we all seem to be chasing after like a pack of hungry hounds after a particularly juicy bone. But what is it, exactly? Is it the feeling you get after eating a particularly delicious meal? Is it the sense of accomplishment you feel after finishing a difficult project at work? Or is it something deeper, more profound? The truth is, satisfaction is a tricky thing to pin down. It's like trying to catch a butterfly with your bare hands – just as you think you have it, it flits away, leaving you with nothing but a handful of air.

But let's be real, who has time for all this introspection and contemplation? We live in a fast-paced world where the only thing that seems to matter is the constant pursuit of more. More money, more success, more stuff. We're all just rats on a never-ending treadmill, running and running but getting nowhere. And yet, despite all this, we still find ourselves searching for satisfaction. We buy the latest gadgets, go on exotic vacations, and indulge in all manner of luxuries, all in the hopes of finding that elusive feeling of contentment. But it never seems to last, does it? We're always left wanting more.

Perhaps the problem is that we're looking for satisfaction in all the wrong places. We're so caught up in the rat race that we've forgotten what truly matters. We've forgotten about the simple things in life – the things that bring us joy and happiness. So, let's take a step back and re-evaluate. Let's forget about all the material possessions and the endless pursuit of success. Let's focus on the things that really matter – our loved ones, our friends, and the memories we make with them. Because at the end of the day, it's not the stuff we accumulate that satisfies us; it's the people we share our lives with. It's the laughter, the love, and the memories we create together. So, let's stop chasing after that butterfly and start cherishing the moments that truly matter.

But let's not stop there, let's also ask ourselves some deeper questions. Are we really satisfied with our lives? Are we really content with our jobs, our relationships, and our material possessions? Or are we just going through the motions, pretending to be satisfied while secretly yearning for something more? And what about all the things we're told we should be satisfied with? The fancy cars, the big houses, and the designer clothing. Are these things really satisfying us, or are they just fleeting distractions from the true emptiness of our lives? And let's not forget about the rat race, the endless pursuit of more, more, more. Are we really satisfied with working ourselves to the bone, sacrificing our health and our relationships, all for the sake of a bigger pay check?

So, are we truly satisfied with our lives? Or are we just living in a world of illusion, where we're told that satisfaction can be found in things that are ultimately empty and meaningless? It's time to take a good, hard look at ourselves and our lives, and ask ourselves the tough questions. Because true satisfaction can only be found by being honest with ourselves and facing the uncomfortable truths about our existence. Now, if you'll excuse me, I'm going to go spend some quality time with my loved ones and maybe even indulge in a nice, juicy bone. Because, as it turns out, satisfaction may be elusive, but it's also right there in front of us if we're willing to see it.

22

Who Am I?

All of us would have asked this question at least once in our lifetime. Who am I?

I've been asking this question to myself for years but alas, couldn't get an answer.

You might say, I'm a human being and I have a name.

So am I my name? No. My name just represents me. I respond when someone calls my name. But I'm not my name.

I breathe air to live, and eat food to survive. So am I air or am I food? No. I'm not air and I'm not food. I only use them to survive. But I'm not them.

I have a life. Am I life? No, life is just a state of being, the moment I lose it, I'll be dead. But whether alive or dead, it's still me. So am I life or death? No.

I have made memories of all the days I've lived so far. I

revisit and cherish those memories. Those memories are what I have made of my life and they define me. So am I memory? No.

I have studied and earned many degrees and do a respectable job for a living. So am I my intellect or knowledge? No, I'm not.

I have an ego and self-respect like everyone else and most of my actions directly or indirectly depend on them. So am I my ego, or am I my self-respect? No. I'm not.

I have a body, a mind and a soul. So am I the body? No. Am I only the soul? No. Am I my mind? No.

I'm not the food, not the air, my knowledge, my body, my pride, my self-respect, and anything that I use every day to define me. I'm still a living being who isn't any of the above but cannot survive without any of the above.

So we are just assembled systems that work with a lot of external support like nature, earth, food, intellect, knowledge, ego, self-respect, friends, relatives, family etc.

Even with all these, we are still nothing, because none of the above defines us completely. The word "I" is not justified by any of the above.

And yet we worry about everything, day in and day out as if our lives are dependent upon it. But we never realize that any of these that we think are extremely important to us are actually not even close to defining us.

I am not the body, I'm not the soul, I'm not anything that I use for this very existence. Who am I then?

We keep saying the word I, me, myself and we strive lifelong to satisfy ourselves and get some respect and stability from that so-called "I".

Who are we? When we don't even know who we are, why are we striving so much to prove ourselves? And run the never-ending cycle of life, study, job, marriage, retirement, and death!

Who am I? Who are you? Why are we running this life-and-death marathon without even knowing who we are and what we are here for?

23

Destiny, Is it predetermined by God?

Destiny, the age-old concept that has been the topic of countless debates and discussions, is the one word that some folks swear by, and others swear it doesn't exist. But what is destiny? Is it something that's predetermined, etched in stone by some higher power? Or is it just an excuse for not taking responsibility for our own lives?

Let's start with the idea that destiny is predetermined. It implies that everything that happens to us, good or bad, is part of a larger plan and that we are just along for the ride. But I mean, come on, are we really just a bunch of marionettes dancing to the whims of fate? Are we just pawns in some grand cosmic game of chess, with destiny as the grandmaster? Are we just players in a game of Monopoly with the bank already owning all the properties? Are we just characters in a choose-your-own-adventure book with the author already deciding the outcome?

If destiny was predetermined, then what's the point of striving for success or working towards our goals? If everything was already decided, then why bother putting in the effort? It's like trying to win a game of Monopoly with the bank already owning all the properties. It's pointless. It's like trying to change the ending of a book that's already been written. It's futile. It's like trying to change the channel on a TV that's not connected to any power source. It's just ridiculous.

But, on the other hand, if destiny is something we create for ourselves, it means that we are the masters of our fate. We have the power to shape our own lives and determine our future. We are the puppet masters of our own lives, pulling the strings and creating our destinies. It means that we are game designers, creating our paths and building our empires. It means that we are the authors of our own lives, writing our own stories and shaping our destinies.

It means that we are in control of our own lives and that we create our destinies through our actions and choices. It's the outcome of the path that we choose to take in life. If we work hard and make good choices, we will create a positive destiny for ourselves. On the other hand, if we make bad choices and take the easy path, we will create a negative destiny. And let's be real, who wants a negative destiny?

So, next time you hear someone spout off about destiny being predetermined, just remember, it's nothing more than a convenient excuse for taking the easy path and not taking responsibility for our own lives. And for all you lazy folks out there, remember, it's always better to be the designer of your own life, not just a player in someone else's game. And if you don't believe me, just ask any Monopoly champion, and they'll tell you the same thing.

But, you might ask, what about those moments when things don't go as planned? What about when life throws us a curveball and we're not prepared for it? Well, that's where the beauty of destiny comes in. Destiny is not only about the outcome but also about the journey. It's about the choices we make, the lessons we learn, and the person we become in the process.

So, go out there and create your destiny, make your own choices, learn your lessons, and become the person you want to be. And remember, it's always good to be the designer and not the player in the game of life.

24

How Much is Too Much in Life

Are you satisfied with the material possessions you currently own? Or do you constantly find yourself wanting more?

Are you content with your current job and career success? Or do you find yourself constantly striving for more power and prestige?

Are you happy with the people in your life? Or do you find yourself searching for something more in your relationships?

Are you comfortable with your current financial situation? Or do you find yourself always working multiple jobs to earn more?

When it comes to the question of "how much is too much in life?" It's a tricky one to answer. Some might say that too much money is when you're swimming in it and can't find your way out, while others might argue that there's no such thing as too much money. But one thing is for sure, it's important to strive for what makes you happy and fulfilled. Whether it's a big house, a fancy car, a high-paying job, or a loving marriage, what's important is that it brings you joy and satisfaction.

However, it's easy to get caught up in societal expectations and the idea that more is always better, and sometimes we forget to appreciate the simple things in life. The moments of laughter with loved ones, the feeling of accomplishment after a hard day's work, the warmth of the sun on your face. These are the things that truly matter and bring true happiness.

It's important to remember that true happiness cannot be bought and it's different for everyone. So, don't compare yourself to others and their choices, focus on what makes you happy. And when you find yourself striving for more, take a moment to appreciate what you already have.

When it comes to your career, remember that it's not just about the money or the title. It's about doing something that you're passionate about and that makes you excited to wake up and go to work every day. And, if you're not happy with your current job, don't be afraid to make a change and pursue something that aligns with your passions and values.

When it comes to your relationships, remember that it's not about the number of people in your life, it's about the quality of those relationships. Surround yourself with people who bring you joy and support you, and don't be afraid to let go of those who hold you back.

In conclusion, don't get caught up in societal expectations and the idea that more is always better. Remember to appreciate the simple things in life and to strive for what truly brings you happiness and fulfilment.

And most importantly, don't forget to have a good laugh along the way, because that's what life is all about. Remember, it's okay to strive for more, but don't forget to enjoy the journey. And when you find yourself questioning "how much is too much in life?" Take a step back, take a deep breath, and remind yourself that happiness is not about having more, it's about being content with what you already have.

One more thing, be kind to yourself and don't be too hard on yourself. It's okay to make mistakes and not have everything figured out. Life is a journey and it's meant to be enjoyed. So, go out there, make your definition of "too much" and live life on your terms. And remember, if anyone tells you that you're doing too much, just tell them to “mind their own business” with a smile.

In the end, it’s all about finding balance and being true to yourself. So, take a moment to reflect on what matters to you, what makes you happy and fulfilled. And remember, you got this.

25

Finding Balance in Life

Are you constantly worrying about whether you're on the right path?

Does everything in your life seem out of balance?

Do you frequently get this thought that you aren't in the right place? Or you aren't doing what you feel like?

Are you adjusting and compromising in your work or personal life?

If yes, you aren't alone. We all have moments of uncertainty and doubt. One of the most important things to keep in mind is that "too much" and "not enough" is often just a matter of perspective. What seems like too much to one person might be just the right amount for another. So, try not to compare yourself to others. Instead, focus on what works for you and what makes you happy.

To find the right balance, it's crucial to understand ourselves and our needs. Reflect on questions like "Are you living according to your values and beliefs? Are you spending your time and energy on things that truly matter to you? Are you taking care of your physical, mental, and emotional well-being? Are you surrounding yourself with people who uplift and support you? Are you taking risks and pursuing your passions? Are you living in the present or constantly worrying about the future or dwelling on the past? Are you sacrificing your happiness for the sake of pleasing others?"

Answering these questions honestly can be difficult, but it's the first step towards finding balance in your life. It's important to remember that finding balance is not a destination, but rather a journey. It's something that you will constantly work on throughout your life. It's okay to make mistakes, and it's okay to fall out of balance at times. The key is to keep reflecting, keep learning, and keep making adjustments as you go along.

Finding a balance between your personal and professional life can be challenging, but it's essential for maintaining your well-being and happiness. Here are a few tips to help you find that balance:

Set clear boundaries: Establish specific times for work and personal activities, and stick to them as much as possible. This will help you avoid burnout and ensure that you're making time for the things that matter to you.

Prioritize self-care: Taking care of your physical, mental, and emotional well-being is crucial for maintaining balance in your life. Make sure you're getting enough sleep, eating well, and making time for exercise and relaxation.

Be mindful of your time: Be mindful of how you're spending your time and energy, and make sure you're not overloading yourself with work or other responsibilities.

Learn to say "no": It's okay to decline invitations or requests if they don't align with your priorities. Saying "no" can help you maintain balance and avoid over-committing.

Communicate with your colleagues: Maintain open communication with your colleagues and managers, and let them know your priorities and availability. This will help you better manage your workload and maintain a balance between work and personal life.

Take breaks: Taking regular breaks throughout the day to disconnect from work, whether it's for a walk, a quick meditation, or just a cup of tea, can help you to refresh your mind and come back to work more focused.

Prioritize your personal relationships: Make time for your family and friends, and don't let work consume all of your time and energy. Nurturing your personal relationships is an essential part of maintaining balance in your life.

Be flexible: Remember that balance is not a fixed state, it's something that you will constantly work on throughout your life. Be flexible and open to change, and adjust your approach as needed.

Finding a balance between personal and professional lives takes effort and requires constant adaptation to the circumstances. But, when you find the right balance, it can make all the difference in terms of your overall well-being and happiness.

Remember, balance is not about perfection; it's about finding a way to live your life that feels good for you. So, take a step back, reflect on your choices and find the right balance that works for you. And remember, it's always okay to make changes and take a different path if something doesn't feel right.

As you reflect, don't be too hard on yourself, and don't be afraid to ask for help if you need it. Life is a journey, and it's about learning and growing as we go along. Embrace the journey, be kind to yourself, and find the balance that works for you. And always remember, whatever you do, don't take life too seriously, it's not like you're getting out alive anyways. And always strive to live a life that is true to yourself, full of passion, happiness, and balance.

26

Life vs Death

Have you ever felt like you've had enough? Like you're done and just want it all to end? I know I have. But here's the thing, death may seem like the ultimate solution to all our problems, but it's not. It's not the end of our struggles, it's not the end of our pain, it's not the end of our regrets. It's just the end of our time here on earth.

And what about life? Have you ever felt like it's just one big struggle? Like you're constantly fighting against the current and not making any progress? I know I have. But here's the thing, life is not meant to be easy, it's meant to be lived. It's meant to be a journey full of ups and downs, twists and turns, laughter and tears. And it's up to us to make the most of it.

I mean, have you ever stopped to think about how you're spending your time? Are you living your best life or just going through the motions? Are you chasing your dreams or just chasing deadlines? Are you making memories or just making a living?

And what about death? Are you waiting for it? Do you spend your days counting down the days until the end? Or are you just going to sit back and let it catch you by surprise?

But here's the thing, death may be the ultimate party crasher, but life is the ultimate wild card. And isn't that what makes life worth living? The unpredictability, the moments that take your breath away, the laughter, the tears, "oh my god moments, I just realized I've been pronouncing ' 'quinoa' wrong."

So, how do we embrace life and accept death? Well, first things first, let's all agree to stop pronouncing "quinoa" wrong. But in all seriousness, the key is to live in the present, to appreciate the moments and people that matter, and to make our mark on the world in a positive way. Each new day is a new life, a new opportunity to make the most of our time here. And let's not waste our time waiting for death, let's focus on making the most of the life we have right now.

In short, let's not waste our time waiting for death, let's make the most of the life we have right now, and have a good laugh while doing it. And always remember that each new day is a new life, a new opportunity to make the most of our time here. So, ask yourself, are you living your life to the fullest? Are you making the most of every opportunity? Are you making the most of your wild card?

And if the answer is no, well then, it's time to make a change; it's time to start living your best life. Because death may be inevitable, but life is a gift, and it's up to us to unwrap it and make the most of it. So, let's not wait for death to come, let's live our lives to the fullest, let's make the most of every opportunity, and let's make the most of our wild card. Let's make the most of the life we have right now, and let's make sure that when death does come knocking at our door, we can say that we've lived a life full of meaning, purpose, and joy.

27

Life is All About Choices

Welcome to the wonderful and confusing world of choices, where every single thing you do is just one decision away. From the mundane, like choosing what to eat for breakfast, to the life-changing, like choosing a career path. But let's not get ahead of ourselves, let's start with the basics.

To wear sweatpants all day or to dress up professionally for a Zoom call?

To eat ice cream with a spoon or with a fork?

To study engineering or medicine?

To pursue a career in a stable industry or to take a risk and start your own business?

To watch a comedy or a drama?

To save money or to spend it on experiences?

To go for a run or to stay in bed and watch Netflix?

To continue in a toxic relationship or to walk away?

To take a public speaking class or to continue avoiding public speaking?

As you can see, some choices may be more serious than others, but they all have the power to shape our lives and shape our future. It's important to consider the consequences of every choice we make and to choose wisely. But it's also important to not take ourselves too seriously and to have fun and enjoy the little things in life.

How do we even make a choice? Well, it's simple really. We weigh the pros and cons, consider the potential outcomes, and then make a decision based on our gut feeling. Sounds easy, right? Wrong. Making choices can be one of the most difficult and overwhelming things in life. It's like trying to choose between a rock and a hard place, or between the devil and the deep blue sea. But fear not, dear reader, for I am here to guide you through the treacherous waters of decision-making.

First things first, let's talk about the pros and cons. Now, I know what you're thinking. "But, isn't that just common sense?" To which I say, "Ha! Common sense is a rare commodity these days." So let me break it down for you. Pros are the good things about a choice, and cons are the bad things. For example, if you're deciding whether or not to eat a doughnut, the pro is that it's delicious, and the con is that it's not exactly healthy. Got it? Good.

Next, let's talk about potential outcomes. This is where things get a little tricky. You see, we can never truly predict what will happen as a result of our choices. Sure, we can make educated guesses, but ultimately, we just have to trust that things will work out in the end. And if they don't? Well, that's just life. It's like rolling the dice and hoping for the best.

Finally, we come to the gut feeling. This is the wild card of decision-making. Some people swear by it, while others think it's a load of nonsense. But here's the thing, your gut feeling is often a reflection of your subconscious. So, if you're feeling uneasy about a choice, it might be worth listening to that little voice in your head.

Let's take a look at a real-life scenario. Imagine you're at a job interview and the interviewer asks you, "why do you want to work for our company?" This, my friends, is a choice. You could say something generic like, "I'm excited about the opportunity to work for such a reputable company," or you could be honest and say, "I need a job, and your company is hiring."

Now, let's weigh the pros and cons. Saying something generic has the pro of making you sound more desirable to the company, but the con is that it's not entirely truthful. Being honest has its pro of being truthful, but the con is that it may make you seem less desirable to the company.

So, what's the potential outcome? If you go with the generic answer, the potential outcome is that you may get the job, but if you're not a good fit, you may end up unhappy in your new position. If you go with the honest answer, the potential outcome is that you may not get the job, but if you do, you'll know that it's the right fit for you. And finally, what does your gut tell you? Do you feel uneasy about not being entirely truthful, or do you feel confident in your honesty?

As you can see, making choices can be a tricky business. But by weighing the pros and cons, considering potential outcomes, and listening to your gut, you can make the best decision for you. So, go forth, and make those choices, big or small. Remember, life is all about taking risks and making mistakes, it's part of the journey. And even if you make the "wrong" choice, it's not the end of the world. It's just an opportunity to learn, grow, and make a better choice next time. So, don't be afraid to take a leap of faith and make a choice, even if it's a difficult one. And if you're ever in doubt, just remember that the only wrong choice is the one you don't make.

Now, as a final note, I want to remind you that, as funny as this may have been, choices are serious business, and you should always be thoughtful and reflective before making any decisions. And most importantly, always be true to yourself, and don't be afraid, to be honest about your intentions and your needs.

So, go out there, make those choices, and don't forget to enjoy the journey!

28

Know Thyself

Hey! I thought you said you loved making fun. Why did you get so upset when he cracked a joke about you?

You said you love a corner seat, but you don't seem to be so happy travelling while sitting in a corner seat today!

I thought you said your favourite colour is green, but you didn't like this green shirt your Mom brought for you?

You must have heard a lot of things like these in your daily life. What do you think? Do you really know who you are? Do you know what your likes and dislikes are?

Knowing oneself is one of the most important things a person can do. After all, if you don't know yourself, how are you supposed to navigate the complicated and often confusing world we live in?

But let's be real here, how much do we really know ourselves? We may think we have a pretty good idea, but the truth is, we often only scratch the surface. We're not as self-aware as we like to think we are. But that's okay because self-discovery is about realizing that we don't know ourselves as well as we thought we did and then taking the time to truly understand ourselves.

Knowing oneself is a crucial step in personal growth and self-improvement, but it's not always easy. We often mistake ourselves for knowing ourselves very well, but in reality, we can be blind to our faults and biases. This can lead us to make false assumptions about ourselves and our abilities.

For example, are you the person you think you are? Do you truly understand your thoughts, feelings, and motivations? Are you aware of your emotional triggers and patterns of behaviour? Are you living in a way that aligns with your values and beliefs?

It's important to question ourselves and our assumptions about ourselves. It's also important to be open-minded and willing to look at our flaws and biases. We should seek feedback from others, practice self-reflection and mindfulness, and be willing to challenge our assumptions about ourselves.

For instance, when someone jokes about us, it's natural to feel upset, but it's important to question whether this reaction is in line with who we think we are. Are we really the type of person who gets easily offended by jokes? Or are we just reacting emotionally without thinking?

But why is self-knowledge so important? For starters, it allows you to understand your thoughts, feelings, and motivations. This understanding can help you make better decisions, set more realistic goals, and improve your relationships with others.

Additionally, knowing oneself can lead to greater self-awareness and self-acceptance. When you understand your strengths and weaknesses, you are less likely to compare yourself to others and more likely to focus on your personal growth. This can lead to a greater sense of self-esteem and self-worth, which in turn can lead to a more fulfilling and satisfying life.

Knowing oneself has many advantages. Some of the key benefits include:

Greater self-awareness: When we know ourselves, we are better able to understand our thoughts, feelings, and motivations. This can help us make better decisions, set more realistic goals, and improve our relationships with others.

Improved self-esteem: Self-knowledge leads to greater self-awareness and self-acceptance, which can lead to a greater sense of self-esteem and self-worth.

Better self-regulation: When we understand our emotional triggers and patterns of behaviour, we are better able to regulate our emotions and manage our reactions to different situations.

Increased authenticity: When we know ourselves, we can be more authentic to ourselves. This can lead to greater satisfaction and fulfilment in life.

However, it's important to note that we often mistake ourselves for knowing ourselves very well. We can be blind to our faults and biases, and this can lead us to make false assumptions about ourselves. This is a common phenomenon known as the "above average effect" or the "Dunning-Kruger effect," which states that people who are incompetent in a certain domain tend to overestimate their abilities.

For example, a person may believe they are a good listener and have strong communication skills, but in reality, they interrupt others frequently or struggle to understand the perspectives of others.

Another example could be someone who thinks they are not affected by stress, but in reality, they have developed unhealthy coping mechanisms like overeating, smoking, or drinking.

But how do you go about "knowing thyself?" Well, it's not always easy, and it's certainly not something that can be accomplished overnight. In fact, self-discovery is a lifelong journey. But there are a few things you can do to get started:

Reflect on your past experiences: Take some time to think about the experiences that have shaped you and the lessons you've learnt from them.

Be honest with yourself: Self-knowledge requires a high degree of honesty and self-awareness. Be willing to look at your flaws and weaknesses and take responsibility for your actions.

Get to know your values: Understand what is important to you and what you stand for.

Try new things: Stepping out of your comfort zone can help you discover new aspects of yourself.

Seek feedback from others: Ask people who know you well for their honest opinions.

Practice mindfulness: Being present and aware of the moment can help you gain insight into your thoughts and emotions.

So, are you ready to take the first step? Are you ready to start peeling back the layers and understanding the real you? Here are a few questions to get you thinking:

Are you willing to look at your flaws and weaknesses, and take responsibility for your actions?

Are you ready to step out of your comfort zone and try new things?

Are you open to receiving honest feedback from others?

Are you willing to practise mindfulness and gain greater self-awareness?

What are your core values and beliefs? Are they aligned with your actions and decision-making?

What are the root causes of your fears and insecurities?

What truly brings you happiness and fulfilment in life?

What are your strengths and weaknesses? Are you utilizing your strengths in your daily life?

What are your long-term life goals?

How do you handle stress?

Are there any patterns or habits that are holding you back?

It's okay if you don't have all the answers right now. Self-discovery is a lifelong journey, and it's important to be consistent with self-reflection, self-awareness, and self-improvement. It's not going to be easy, but it will be worth it.

So, go forth and discover yourself, embrace the process, and enjoy the journey of learning and growing as an individual. Remember, it's not like you're going to find a secret treasure or anything, but you'll find the treasure of self-knowledge and acceptance, and that's truly invaluable.

29

What's Beyond Life?

Seconds go by in a blink, minutes ratify by as you think, hours, and then days and years… and finally, a lifetime slips away before you even realize it.

Being born is sure a mystery. Dying is too. What happens in between is a bigger mystery than life and death itself. But, ironically, we live in that mystery as if we have mastered it. Yet deep down, we wonder why this is the way it is.

Our entire lives, every single event is something we have designed and created within our minds or someone else's minds. And the day-to-day events are the consequences of those choices. Do you agree?

I wanted to start my business, it's my desire. I have created a plan, taken progressive steps, and today I am the CEO! But whatever that's happening in my life, after starting the business – could it be money, fame, legal issues, family issues, success, or failure? Aren't they all the consequences of the very decision that I took of becoming a business owner?

This simplifies that we are in total control of our lives. Our destiny is just the aftermath of our decisions which stemmed out of our desire to do or to be or to want something.

Whatever this life is on earth that you and I are living, it is driven by just one force DESIRE!

Desire to live, desire to possess something better, desire to get a better job, desire to live a luxurious life. Every action we ever took, is because of the force called desire.

Do you agree with me on this point?

If you can understand the above statement, I guess you can understand that the whole life on earth is manifested because of the different desires of different people, animals, or even plants and tiny creatures.

One person's desire becomes another person's destiny. One animal's desire to live becomes another animal's death. One couple's desire to parent becomes another new life. One person's desire becomes start-ups and multinational companies. The desire for power is destroying nations in name of war, the same desire to explore is taking us to the moon and Mars.

What not can desire do? After all, we all are living because of this desire.

Is desire good or bad?

It's absolutely good! Because without it, the very world we live in would cease!

If the desire is so powerful, and if each one of us possesses this immense treasure that is helping us manifest the life we want, why not use this powerful tool for something extraordinary?

Desiring a car, house, children, health, and wealth is extremely common. We have all been doing that since times immemorial and we have all succeeded in achieving these simple things.

Why don't we go the extra mile? Why don't we desire to understand what the essence of this very life is?

God has created us. Agreed. But did he just create us so that we fall into this unending loop of life, desire, death, and rebirth? Isn't there anything beyond this mundane life that billions of people have been living repeatedly for thousands of years?

There should be something that we are failing to understand. Don't you think?

Come on, won't God be bored of seeing us live this vicious circle of birth and death with desire driving us in between?

If God is such a powerful ultimatum who created us, why should his human creation be this simple, boring, and self-repetitive?

Don't you think there is more to just birth and death and life in between? A dimension that not many of us have explored yet?

You might say that saints and sadhus, or gurus have explored and attained mukti or liberation. And it is ultimately our purpose and once we attain mukti, we will become one with God.

Now I'm not talking about mukti or liberation, because it's just another desire. A desire to be with God.

Come on guys, why would God want such useless creatures like us to attain mukti and be one with him? Doesn't make sense right? We were not able to understand the very purpose of why God sent us to earth, and wasted all our lives in this vicious circle finally realizing this life is worthless and then we seek mukti and ask God to take us back!

Nope! Doesn't seem the right way to me! At least if we would have fulfilled one of his purposes on earth while we are here, it's fair enough to ask him to give us mukti and take us back since we have achieved our purpose.

But that's not what is happening here. After wasting the majority of our life fulfilling desires, probably in our old age or when we know this life is about to end, we read a few scriptures and desire instant mukti!

Think deeper, we are not looking for mukti here, it's again a desire after all. We are seeking enlightenment. The very purpose of us being on earth.

We all firmly believe that we are sent by God onto this earth. Right?

What if this birth, life, death, and rebirth are not the purpose after all?

What if we were part of a bigger mission of God and this time on earth is just a layover?

A layover for us to learn, understand and equip ourselves to take our next flight (via death) to reach our next destination to fulfil God's mission.

But what should we learn during our time on earth is something we got to figure out.

In the meantime,

What if?

Just give it a thought!

what do you think is our purpose in life?

30

Goodbyes Are Byes for Good

Goodbye, goodbye, goodbye. The word that strikes fear in the hearts of many. The word that represents the end of something. The word that makes us feel like we're losing something. But you know what? Goodbye doesn't have to be a bad thing. In fact, it can be a good thing. It can be a way to start something new, to move on to bigger and better things.

Think about it. When you say goodbye to a job that you hate, you're opening yourself up to new opportunities. When you say goodbye to a relationship that isn't working, you're freeing yourself to find someone who will treat you right. And when you say goodbye to a friend who is holding you back, you're making room for new friendships that will help you grow.

So, my dear friends, don't be afraid of goodbye. Embrace it. Embrace the change and the new possibilities that come with it. And if you're worried about staying in touch with the person or company you're saying goodbye to, don't be. Just because you're not working together or seeing each other every day, doesn't mean you can't still have a relationship.

In fact, sometimes distance can make the heart grow fonder. You'll appreciate the time you do have together even more. Plus, with technology, it's easier than ever to stay in touch. You can message, call, video chat, and even send virtual hugs if you want.

So, don't be sad when you say goodbye. Be excited. Be excited for what's to come. And remember, just because you're saying goodbye to one thing, doesn't mean you're saying goodbye to everything. It's just a bye for the greater good.

So go forth, my friends, and say goodbye with confidence and a smile on your face. Because you never know, the next person or opportunity you meet might just be the best thing that ever happened to you.

And one final thing, just because you say goodbye, it doesn't mean the door is closed forever, it can be opened again when the time is right. So, keep the key of your heart with you, you never know when you might need it.

Goodbye, my dear friends. But only for now. I'll see you again with another book shortly. Until then, keep missing me.

www.ingramcontent.com/pod-product-compliance
Lightning Source LLC
LaVergne TN
LVHW041219150826
845673LV00001B/458

* 9 7 9 8 8 8 9 3 5 8 9 4 7 *